D0128344

THE AUSTRALIAN
Women's Weekly
slow cooker

acp
books

Contents

The oven temperatures in this book are for fan-forced ovens. If you have a conventional oven, increase the temperature by 10-20 degrees. The imperial measurements used in these recipes are approximate only and should not affect your cooking results. A conversion chart appears on the inside cover flap.

Take it slowly

Getting the best from your slow cooker

There's something wonderful about the aroma, flavour and texture of a slow-cooked meal. Slow cookers are perfect for this way of cooking. First, read the manufacturer's instruction manual carefully, it will advise you to NOT leave the appliance on and unattended at any time; this, of course, is a safety measure.

These appliances are available in various shapes and sizes, and with a host of different features. For example, some have timers that cut off after the cooking time has expired, some don't; some have timers that reduce the temperature and keep the food warm until you decide to eat. If you're in the market for a slow cooker, research the subject fully: check out the cookers and their features carefully to make sure the appliance suits your needs. They are all "safe" in terms of making sure the food reaches the correct temperatures to destroy any harmful bacteria during the long slow cooking times.

We chose to test the recipes in this cookbook using a 4.5 litre (10 cup) slow cooker, the most popular size. If you have a smaller or larger slow cooker than the one we used, you will have to decrease or increase the quantity of food, and almost certainly the liquid content, in the recipes.

Handy hints

Most recipes using red meat recommend that the meat is browned first, as if you were making a casserole. Do this in a heated oiled large frying pan, adding the meat in batches, and turning the meat so it browns all over. Over-crowding the pan will result in stewed, not browned, meat. If you're pushed for time, the meat and/or vegetables can be browned the night before. Once everything is browned, put it into a sealable container, along with any juices, and refrigerate until the next day. Some recipes suggest tossing the meat in flour before browning, some don't. Usually when the meat is floured, the finished sauce will be thick enough to make a light coating gravy. If the meat is not floured, it might be necessary to thicken the sauce. Usually plain flour or cornflour are used for thickening; cornflour results in a less-cloudy sauce than if flour is used. The flour, or cornflour, needs to be blended with

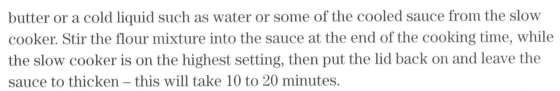

butter or a cold liquid such as water or some of the cooled sauce from the slow cooker. Stir the flour mixture into the sauce at the end of the cooking time, while the slow cooker is on the highest setting, then put the lid back on and leave the sauce to thicken – this will take 10 to 20 minutes.

As a general rule for casserole, stew, curry and tagine recipes, the container of the slow cooker should be at least half-full. Place the vegetables into the cooker, put the meat on top of the vegetables, then add the liquid. Soups are easy, just make sure the cooker is at least half-full. Roasts, using whole pieces of meat or poultry and pot roasts are sometimes cooked with hardly any liquid – especially if the meat is cooking on a bed of vegetables – sometimes a little liquid is added simply to make a sauce or gravy. Corned meats are usually cooked in enough liquid to barely cover them.

Some meats produce a lot of fat if cooked over a long period of time. There are a couple of gadgets available in kitchen/cookware shops for removing fat: one is a type of "brush" that sweeps away the fat; the other is a type of jug that separates the fat from the liquid. However, one of the easiest ways to remove fat is to soak it up using sheets of absorbent kitchen paper on the surface. The best way of all is to refrigerate the food, the fat will set on top of the liquid, then it can simply be lifted off and discarded.

Freezing leftovers

Each recipe notes if it is suitable to freeze or not. The slow cooker's capacity allows you to cook quite a lot of food at once, so if there's any left over, it's smart to freeze some for another time. There is always a lot of liquid to contend with in the slow cooker, so remove the meat and vegetables to appropriate-sized freezer-friendly containers, pour in enough of the liquid to barely cover the meat etc, seal the container, and freeze – while it's hot is fine – for up to three months. Any leftover liquid can be frozen separately and used as a base for another recipe, such as soup or a sauce.

What setting do I use?

Use the low setting for a long, all-day, cooking time, or reduce the cooking time by about half if using the high setting. The food will reach simmering point on either setting. If your slow cooker has a warm setting, this is not used for actual cooking; it's used after the cooking time to maintain the food's temperature until you're ready to eat.

If you need to add ingredients or thicken the sauce after the cooking time, turn the covered slow cooker to high to get maximum heat. Remove the lid and add the ingredients or thickening, replace the lid and leave the cooker to heat the added ingredients or to thicken the sauce; this will take between 10 and 20 minutes.

Can I use any of my favourite recipes in a slow cooker?

Most soup, stew, casserole, tagine and curry recipes are perfect to use in the slow cooker. The trick is to make sure there is enough liquid in the cooker for the long, slow, cooking time. Once you get to know the cooker, you'll be able to adapt a lot of your favourite recipes. Some roasts work well in the slow cooker, too. Use recipes that you would normally slow cook, well-covered in an oven set at a low temperature. Also, some conventionally slow-cooked desserts, and steamed pudding recipes can be used in the slow cooker.

What cuts of meat should I use?

Use secondary, cheaper, tougher cuts of red meat. The long, slow, cooking time will tenderise the cuts, and the flavours will be excellent; it's simply a waste to use more expensive primary cuts for this method of cooking. Other types of meat (secondary/stewing cuts) such as venison, goat, rabbit, hare, kangaroo etc, are suitable to use in the slow cooker.

All kinds of poultry cook well in a slow cooker; but be careful not to overcook it, as it will become stringy. If you can access mature birds, such as boiling fowls or wild duck etc, the long, slow cooking times will tenderise the flesh making it very flavoursome. Seafood is generally not suitable to use in a slow cooker as it toughens quickly. However, there are many recipes for sauces that marry well with seafood, and these can be cooked in the slow cooker, and the seafood added just before you're ready to serve. Large octopus will cook and become tender in a slow cooker.

Important safety tips

Read the instruction manual of the appliance carefully.

Make sure the cooker is sitting flat on the bench well away from water, any heat source, such as gas flames, stove tops and ovens, curtains, walls, children and pets.

Make sure the electrical cord is well away from any water or heat source, and make sure the cord is not dangling on the floor, as someone might trip on it.

Make sure no one touches any metal part of the cooker while it's in use, as the metal parts do get very hot.

General cleaning

Most slow cooker inserts can be washed in hot soapy water. To remove cooked-on food, soak in warm water, then scrub lightly with a plastic or nylon brush. Never put a hot insert under cold water, as this can cause the insert to break. The outer metal container should never be placed in water; just wipe the outside with a damp cloth and dry. Don't use abrasives or chemicals to clean the cooker, as these can damage the surfaces.

A note on dried beans

We have used canned beans in this cookbook, but should you want to use dried beans instead, there are few things you must do to prevent food poisoning.

All kidney-shaped beans of all colours and sizes, are related to each other and must be washed, drained, then boiled in fresh water until they're tender – there's no need for overnight soaking; the time depends on the type of bean. Then, like canned beans, they can be added to the food in the slow cooker.

Soya beans and chickpeas are fine to use raw in the slow cooker, just rinse them well first; there's no need for overnight soaking before cooking them in the slow cooker.

Soup

lamb shank, fennel and vegetable soup

serves 6

1 tablespoon olive oil
4 french-trimmed lamb shanks (1kg)
1 medium brown onion (150g), chopped coarsely
2 baby fennel bulbs (260g), sliced thinly
2 medium carrots (240g), chopped coarsely
4 cloves garlic, crushed
2 fresh small red thai (serrano) chillies, chopped finely
2 teaspoons ground cumin
2 teaspoons ground coriander
1 teaspoon ground cinnamon
1 teaspoon caraway seeds
pinch saffron threads
1.5 litres (6 cups) water
2 cups (500ml) beef stock
400g (14½ ounces) canned diced tomatoes
400g (15 ounces) canned chickpeas (garbanzo beans), rinsed, drained
¾ cup (90g) frozen baby peas
1 cup loosely packed fresh coriander (cilantro) leaves

1 Heat half the oil in large frying pan; cook lamb, until browned all over, then place in 4.5-litre (18-cup) slow cooker.
2 Heat remaining oil in same pan; cook onion, fennel, carrot, garlic and chilli, stirring, until onion softens. Add spices; cook, stirring, until fragrant. Place vegetable mixture into cooker. Stir in the water, stock, undrained tomatoes and chickpeas. Cook, covered, on low, 10 hours.
3 Remove lamb from cooker. When cool enough to handle, remove meat from bones, shred meat; discard bones. Stir meat, peas and coriander leaves into cooker. Season to taste.

prep + cook time 10 hours 30 minutes
nutritional count per serving 6.1g total fat (1.4g saturated fat); 953kJ (228 cal); 13.6g carbohydrate; 26.3g protein; 6.7g fibre

serving suggestion Serve soup with lemon wedges, greek-style yogurt and crusty bread.

• suitable to freeze at the end of step 2.

italian chicken soup

serves 6

1.5kg (3 pound) chicken
3 large tomatoes (650g)
1 medium brown onion (150g), chopped coarsely
2 stalks celery (300g), trimmed, chopped coarsely
1 large carrot (180g), chopped coarsely
2 dried bay leaves
4 cloves garlic, peeled, halved
6 black peppercorns
2 litres (8 cups) water
¾ cup (155g) risoni pasta
½ cup coarsely chopped fresh flat-leaf parsley
½ cup coarsely chopped fresh basil
2 tablespoons finely chopped fresh oregano
¼ cup (60ml) fresh lemon juice

1 Discard as much skin as possible from chicken.
Chop 1 tomato coarsely. Chop remaining tomatoes
finely; refrigerate, covered, until required.
2 Place chicken, coarsely chopped tomato, onion,
celery, carrot, bay leaves, garlic, peppercorns and
the water in 4.5-litre (18-cup) slow cooker. Cook,
covered, on low, 8 hours.

3 Carefully remove chicken from cooker. Strain
broth through fine sieve into large heatproof bowl;
discard solids. Skim and discard any fat from broth.
Return broth to cooker; add risoni and finely chopped
tomatoes. Cook, covered, on high, about 30 minutes
or until risoni is tender.
4 Meanwhile, when cool enough to handle, remove
meat from bones; shred coarsely. Discard bones.
Add chicken, herbs and juice to soup; cook, covered,
on high, 5 minutes. Season to taste.

prep + cook time 9 hours
nutritional count per serving 14.1g total fat
(4.4g saturated fat); 1580kJ (378 cal);
23.2g carbohydrate; 37g protein; 4.5g fibre

• suitable to freeze at the end of step 2.

borscht

60g (2 ounces) butter
2 medium brown onions (300g), chopped finely
500g (1 pound) beef chuck steak, cut into
　large chunks
1 cup (250ml) water
750g (1½ pounds) beetroot (beets), peeled,
　chopped finely
2 medium potatoes (400g), chopped finely
2 medium carrots (240g), chopped finely
4 small (360g) finely chopped tomatoes
1 litre (4 cups) beef stock
⅓ cup (80ml) red wine vinegar
3 dried bay leaves
4 cups (320g) finely shredded cabbage
2 tablespoons coarsely chopped fresh
　flat-leaf parsley
½ cup (120g) sour cream

1 Melt half the butter in large frying pan; cook onion, stirring, until soft. Place onion in 4.5-litre (18-cup) slow cooker. Melt remaining butter in same pan; cook beef, stirring, until browned all over. Place beef in cooker. Add the water to the same pan; bring to the boil, then add beetroot, potato, carrot, tomato, stock, vinegar and bay leaves to slow cooker. Cook, covered, on low, 8 hours.
2 Discard bay leaves. Remove beef from soup; shred using two forks. Return beef to soup with cabbage; cook, covered, on high, about 20 minutes or until cabbage is wilted. Stir in parsley.
3 Serve soup topped with sour cream.

prep + cook time 8 hours 50 minutes
nutritional count per serving 20.6g total fat
(12.4g saturated fat); 1689kJ (404 cal);
25.3g carbohydrate; 25.3g protein; 8.8g fibre

• suitable to freeze at the end of step 1.

cream of celeriac soup

serves 6

2kg (4 pounds) celeriac (celery root),
  chopped coarsely
1 medium brown onion (150g), chopped coarsely
3 cloves garlic, quartered
1 stalk celery (150g), trimmed, chopped coarsely
1.5 litres (6 cups) water
1 litre (4 cups) chicken stock
½ cup (125ml) pouring cream
⅓ cup loosely packed fresh chervil leaves
1 tablespoon olive oil

1 Combine celeriac, onion, garlic, celery, the water
and stock in 4.5-litre (18-cup) slow cooker. Cook,
covered, on low, 8 hours.
2 Stand soup 10 minutes, then blend or process,
in batches, until smooth. Return soup to cooker;
stir in cream. Cook, covered, on high, until hot;
season to taste.
3 Serve soup sprinkled with chervil; drizzle with oil.

prep + cook time 8 hours 30 minutes
nutritional count per serving 13.3g total fat
(6.7g saturated fat); 995kJ (238 cal);
16.8g carbohydrate; 7.1g protein; 12.6g fibre

tip Be careful when blending or processing hot
soup – don't over-fill the container (one-third to
half-full as a guide), and make sure the lid is secure.

• suitable to freeze at the end of step 1.

spicy red lentil and chickpea soup

2 teaspoons vegetable oil
1 medium brown onion (150g), chopped finely
2 cloves garlic, crushed
2.5cm (1 inch) piece fresh ginger (15g), grated
2 teaspoons smoked paprika
1 teaspoon ground cumin
½ teaspoon dried chilli flakes
375g (12 ounces) pumpkin, chopped coarsely
1 stalk celery (150g), trimmed, sliced thickly
¾ cup (150g) red lentils
400g (15 ounces) canned chickpeas
  (garbanzo beans), rinsed, drained
400g (14½ ounces) canned diced tomatoes
3 cups (750ml) water
3 cups (750ml) vegetable stock
⅓ cup (80ml) finely chopped fresh flat-leaf parsley

1   Heat oil in small frying pan; cook onion, garlic and ginger, stirring, until onion softens. Add spices and chilli; cook, stirring, until fragrant.
2   Place onion mixture into 4.5-litre (18-cup) slow cooker; stir in pumpkin, celery, lentils, chickpeas, undrained tomatoes, the water and stock. Cook, covered, on low, 6 hours. Season to taste.
3   Serve soup sprinkled with parsley.

prep + cook time 6 hours 20 minutes
nutritional count per serving 3.9g total fat
(0.8g saturated fat); 815kJ (195 cal);
23.5g carbohydrate; 12.4g protein; 7.9g fibre

• suitable to freeze at the end of step 2.

ribollita

serves 6

1 ham hock (1kg)
1 medium brown onion (150g), chopped finely
2 stalks celery (300g), trimmed, sliced thinly
1 large carrot (180g), chopped finely
1 small fennel bulb (200g), sliced thinly
3 cloves garlic, crushed
400g (14½ ounces) canned diced tomatoes
2 sprigs fresh rosemary
½ teaspoon dried chilli flakes
2 litres (8 cups) water
375g (12 ounces) cavolo nero, shredded coarsely
400g (15 ounces) canned cannellini beans,
  rinsed, drained
½ cup coarsely chopped fresh basil
250g (½ pound) sourdough bread, crust removed
½ cup (40g) flaked parmesan cheese

1 Combine hock, onion, celery, carrot, fennel, garlic, undrained tomatoes, rosemary, chilli and the water in 4.5-litre (18-cup) slow cooker. Cook, covered, on low, 8 hours.
2 Remove hock from cooker; add cavolo nero and beans to soup. Cook, covered, on high, about 20 minutes or until cavolo nero is wilted.
3 Meanwhile, when hock is cool enough to handle, remove meat from bone; shred coarsely. Discard skin, fat and bone. Add meat and basil to soup; season to taste.
4 Break chunks of bread into serving bowls; top with soup and cheese.

prep + cook time 8 hours 45 minutes
nutritional count per serving 4.9g total fat (2.1g saturated fat); 798kJ (191 cal); 18g carbohydrate; 15.1g protein; 7g fibre

• suitable to freeze at the end of step 1.

tip Ribollita [ree-boh-lee-tah] literally means 'reboiled'. This famous Tuscan soup was originally made by reheating leftover minestrone or vegetable soup and adding chunks of bread, white beans and other vegetables such as carrot, zucchini, spinach and cavolo nero.

pork and fennel soup

serves 6

500g (1 pound) piece pork neck
4 small potatoes (500g), chopped coarsely
2 large fennel bulbs (1kg), chopped coarsely
 (see tip)
1 medium brown onion (150g), chopped coarsely
2 cloves garlic, quartered
1 dried bay leaf
6 black peppercorns
1.5 litres (6 cups) water
2 cups (500ml) chicken stock
½ cup (125ml) pouring cream

1 Tie pork at 2.5cm (1 inch) intervals with kitchen string. Combine the pork, potato, fennel, onion, garlic, bay leaf, peppercorns, the water and stock in 4.5-litre (18-cup) slow cooker. Cook, covered, on low, 6 hours.
2 Discard bay leaf. Transfer pork to medium bowl; remove string. Using two forks, shred pork coarsely.

3 Stand soup 10 minutes, then blend or process, in batches, until smooth. Return soup to cooker; stir in cream. Cook, covered, on high, until hot. Season to taste.
4 Serve soup topped with pork and reserved fennel fronds.

prep + cook time 6 hours 40 minutes
nutritional count per serving 16.2g total fat (8.4g saturated fat); 1258kJ (301 cal); 14.9g carbohydrate; 22g protein; 4.3g fibre

tip Reserve some of the feathery fennel fronds to sprinkle over the soup at serving time.

• suitable to freeze at the end of step 1. Thaw and reheat soup, then shred pork.

pea and ham soup

serves 6

500g (1 pound) green split peas
1 tablespoon olive oil
1 large brown onion (200g), chopped finely
3 cloves garlic, crushed
1 ham hock (1kg)
2 medium carrots (240g), chopped finely
2 stalks celery (300g), trimmed, chopped finely
4 fresh thyme sprigs
2 dried bay leaves
2 litres (8 cups) water

1   Rinse peas under cold water until water runs clear; drain.
2   Heat oil in large frying pan; cook onion and garlic, stirring, until onion softens. Place onion mixture into 4.5-litre (18-cup) slow cooker; stir in peas and remaining ingredients. Cook, covered, on low, 8 hours.
3   Remove ham from cooker. When cool enough to handle, remove meat from bone; shred coarsely, return meat to slow cooker. Discard skin, fat and bone. Season soup to taste.

prep + cook time 8 hours 20 minutes
nutritional count per serving 6.4g total fat
(1.2g saturated fat); 1517kJ (363 cal);
43g carbohydrate; 27.3g protein; 11g fibre

serving suggestion Serve soup topped with coarsely chopped mint leaves, thinly sliced green onions (scallions) and greek-style yogurt.

• suitable to freeze at the end of step 2.

cuban black bean soup

serves 6

1½ cups (300g) dried black turtle beans
1 ham hock (1kg)
2 tablespoons olive oil
1 large brown onion (200g), chopped finely
1 medium red capsicum (bell pepper) (200g),
  chopped finely
3 garlic cloves, crushed
3 teaspoons ground cumin
1 teaspoon dried chilli flakes
400g (14½ ounces) canned crushed tomatoes
2 litres (8 cups) water
3 teaspoons dried oregano leaves
1 teaspoon ground black pepper
2 tablespoons lime juice
1 large tomato (220g), chopped finely
¼ cup coarsely chopped fresh coriander (cilantro)

1 Place beans in medium bowl, cover with cold water; stand overnight.
2 Drain and rinse beans, place in medium saucepan, cover with cold water; bring to the boil. Boil, uncovered, 15 minutes; drain.
3 Meanwhile, preheat oven to 200°C/400°F.
4 Roast ham on oven tray for 30 minutes.
5 Heat oil in large frying pan; cook onion, capsicum and garlic, stirring, until onion is soft. Add cumin and chilli; cook, stirring, until fragrant.
6 Combine beans, ham, onion mixture, undrained tomatoes, the water, oregano and pepper in 4.5-litre (18-cup) slow cooker. Cook, covered, on low, 8 hours.
7 Remove ham from cooker. When cool enough to handle, remove meat from bone; shred coarsely. Discard skin, fat and bone. Blend or process 2 cups soup mixture until smooth. Return meat to cooker with pureed soup, stir in juice and tomato; sprinkle with coriander. Season to taste.

prep + cook time 8 hours 55 minutes (+ standing)
nutritional count per serving 18.1g total fat (2.9g saturated fat); 1350kJ (323 cal); 9.6g carbohydrate; 24.7g protein; 12.4g fibre

• suitable to freeze at the end of step 6.

asian noodle soup

1kg (2 pounds) chicken necks
1 medium brown onion (150g), chopped coarsely
1 stalk celery (150g), trimmed, chopped coarsely
1 medium carrot (120g), chopped coarsely
2 dried bay leaves
1 teaspoon black peppercorns
2.5 litres (10 cups) water
2 tablespoons tamari
2.5 cm (1 inch) piece fresh ginger (10g),
　shredded finely
250g (8 ounces) dried ramen noodles
220g (7 ounces) japanese tofu
1 tablespoon vegetable oil
90g (3 ounces) fresh shiitake mushrooms,
　sliced thinly
2 baby buk choy (300g), chopped coarsely
60g (2 ounces) enoki mushrooms
2 green onions (scallions), sliced thinly

1 Combine chicken, onion, celery, carrot, bay leaves, peppercorns and the water in 4.5-litre (18-cup) slow cooker. Cook, covered, on low, 8 hours.
2 Strain stock through fine sieve into large heatproof bowl; discard solids.
3 Return stock to cooker; add tamari and ginger. Cook, uncovered, on high, about 20 minutes or until hot. Season to taste.
4 Meanwhile, cook noodles in medium saucepan of boiling water until tender; drain. Divide noodles into serving bowls. Chop tofu into cubes.
5 Heat oil in same pan; cook shiitake mushrooms, stirring, until browned all over. Divide shiitake mushrooms, tofu, buk choy, enoki mushrooms, green onions and hot stock between serving bowls.

prep + cook time 8 hours 50 minutes
nutritional count per serving 6.2g total fat
(0.8g saturated fat); 1012kJ (242 cal);
32.4g carbohydrate; 11.4g protein; 5.1g fibre

• suitable to freeze at the end of step 1.

pumpkin soup

serves 6

30g (1 ounce) butter
1 tablespoon olive oil
1 large leek (500g), sliced thinly
1.8kg (3¾ pound) piece pumpkin,
  chopped coarsely
1 large potato (300g), chopped coarsely
3 cups (750ml) chicken stock
3 cups (750ml) water
½ cup (125ml) pouring cream
1 tablespoon finely chopped fresh chives

1 Heat butter and oil in large frying pan; cook leek, stirring, until soft.
2 Combine leek mixture, pumpkin, potato, stock and the water in 4.5-litre (18-cup) slow cooker. Cook, covered, on low, 6 hours.
3 Cool soup 10 minutes. Blend or process soup, in batches, until smooth. Return soup to cooker. Cook, covered, on high, about 20 minutes or until hot. Stir in ⅓ cup of the cream. Season to taste.
4 Serve soup topped with remaining cream and chives.

prep + cook time 6 hours 30 minutes
nutritional count per serving 17.9g total fat (10.1g saturated fat); 1275kJ (305 cal); 24.8g carbohydrate; 9g protein; 5.1g fibre

• suitable to freeze at the end of step 2.

Stews & Casseroles

spicy tomato and saffron chicken casserole serves 6

¼ cup (35g) plain (all-purpose) flour
2 tablespoons moroccan seasoning
6 chicken thigh cutlets (1.2kg)
1 tablespoon vegetable oil
1 large brown onion (200g), sliced thickly
2 cloves garlic, crushed
2.5cm (1 inch) piece fresh ginger (15g), grated
1 fresh long red chilli, sliced thinly
2 cups (500ml) chicken stock
400g (14½ ounces) canned diced tomatoes
¼ cup (70g) tomato paste
¼ teaspoon saffron threads
PRESERVED LEMON GREMOLATA
⅓ cup finely chopped fresh flat-leaf parsley
1 tablespoon thinly sliced preserved
   lemon rind
1 clove garlic, crushed

1 Combine flour and 1 tablespoon of the seasoning in small shallow bowl; toss chicken in flour mixture to coat, shake off excess. Heat half the oil in large frying pan; cook chicken, in batches, until browned. Transfer to 4.5-litre (18-cup) slow cooker.
2 Heat remaining oil in same pan, add onion, garlic, ginger, chilli and remaining seasoning; cook, stirring, until onion softens. Add ½ cup of the stock; cook, stirring, until mixture boils.
3 Stir onion mixture into cooker with remaining stock, undrained tomatoes, paste and saffron. Cook, covered, on low, 6 hours. Season to taste.
4 Make preserved lemon gremolata before serving.
5 Sprinkle casserole with gremolata.
preserved lemon gremolata Combine ingredients in small bowl.

prep + cook time 6 hours 25 minutes
nutritional count per serving 23.8g total fat (7.2g saturated fat); 1522kJ (364 cal); 10.2g carbohydrate; 26.5g protein; 2.5g fibre

tip Preserved lemon is available at delicatessens and some supermarkets. Remove and discard the flesh, wash the rind, then use it as the recipe directs.
serving suggestion Serve casserole with steamed rice or couscous.

• suitable to freeze at the end of step 3.

balsamic and port beef shanks

serves 6

1 tablespoon olive oil
1.8kg (3¾ pound) piece beef shank,
  cut into 6 pieces
1 large red onion (300g), sliced thickly
1 stalk celery (150g), trimmed, sliced thickly
½ cup (125ml) beef stock
½ cup (125ml) port
¼ cup (60ml) balsamic vinegar
400g (14½ ounces) canned diced tomatoes
2 sprigs fresh thyme
1 tablespoon light brown sugar
⅓ cup coarsely chopped fresh basil
2 teaspoons finely grated lemon rind
½ cup (60g) seeded black olives

1 Heat oil in large frying pan; cook beef, in batches, until browned. Transfer to 4.5-litre (18-cup) slow cooker. Add onion, celery, stock, port, vinegar, undrained tomatoes, thyme and sugar to slow cooker; cook, covered, on low, 8 hours.
2 Stir in basil, rind and olives; season to taste.
3 Serve beef with sauce.

prep + cook time 8 hours 20 minutes
nutritional count per serving 16.3g total fat
(5.9g saturated fat); 1726kJ (413 cal);
12.1g carbohydrate; 48.2g protein; 1.9g fibre

tips Ask the butcher to cut the beef shank into 6 equal pieces for you, or you could use 6 x 300g (10 ounce) pieces beef osso buco. Dry red wine can be used instead of port.
serving suggestion Serve shanks with risotto, mashed potato or soft polenta.

• suitable to freeze at the end of step 1.

chilli con carne

serves 6

1 tablespoon olive oil
1 large brown onion (200g), chopped finely
2 cloves garlic, crushed
750g (1½ pounds) minced (ground) beef
1 teaspoon ground cumin
1½ teaspoons dried chilli flakes
1 cup (250ml) beef stock
⅓ cup (95g) tomato paste
820g (28 ounces) canned crushed tomatoes
1 tablespoon finely chopped fresh oregano
800g (30 ounces) canned kidney beans,
   rinsed, drained
½ cup loosely packed fresh coriander
   (cilantro) leaves
6 flour tortillas, warmed

serving suggestion Serve chilli con carne with
steamed rice and a dollop of sour cream, plus
a green leafy salad.

• suitable to freeze at the end of step 1.

1 Heat oil in large frying pan; cook onion and
garlic, stirring, until onion softens. Add beef, cumin
and chilli; cook, stirring, until browned. Transfer to
4.5-litre (18-cup) slow cooker. Stir in stock, paste,
undrained tomatoes and oregano. Cook, covered,
on low, 8 hours.
2 Add beans; cook, covered, on high, about
30 minutes or until hot. Season to taste.
3 Sprinkle chilli con carne with coriander; serve
with tortillas.

prep + cook time 8 hours 45 minutes
nutritional count per serving 14.8g total fat
(5.4g saturated fat); 1743kJ (417 cal);
30.9g carbohydrate; 35.1g protein; 9.5g fibre

corned beef with horseradish sauce

serves 6

1.5kg (3¼ pound) piece corned silverside
1 medium brown onion (150g), chopped coarsely
1 medium carrot (120g), chopped coarsely
1 stalk celery (150g), trimmed, chopped coarsely
10 black peppercorns
1 tablespoon brown malt vinegar
1 teaspoon light brown sugar
2.5 litres (10 cups) water, approximately
HORSERADISH SAUCE
45g (1½ ounces) butter
2 tablespoons plain (all-purpose) flour
2 cups (500ml) hot milk
1 tablespoon horseradish cream
1 tablespoon coarsely chopped fresh
   flat-leaf parsley

1 Rinse beef under cold water; pat dry with absorbent paper. Place beef, onion, carrot, celery, peppercorns, vinegar and sugar in 4.5-litre (18-cup) slow cooker. Add enough of the water to barely cover beef. Cook, covered, on low, 8 hours.
2 Make horseradish sauce just before serving.
3 Remove beef from cooker; discard liquid and vegetables.
4 Slice beef thickly; serve with horseradish sauce.
horseradish sauce Melt butter in medium saucepan, add flour; cook, stirring, 1 minute. Gradually add milk, stirring, until sauce boils and thickens. Stir in horseradish cream and parsley. Season to taste.

prep + cook time 8 hours 10 minutes
nutritional count per serving 26.1g total fat
(13.9g saturated fat); 2266kJ (542 cal);
10.2g carbohydrate; 65.7g protein; 1.4g fibre

• not suitable to freeze.

serving suggestion A mixture of steamed seasonal vegetables make a good accompaniment to corned beef. Try baby potatoes, carrots, peas or beans, squash or zucchini.

artichokes with garlic anchovy crumbs   serves 6 [as a starter]

6 medium globe artichokes (1.2kg)
2 litres (8 cups) water
2 cups (500ml) chicken stock
2 tablespoons lemon juice
¼ cup (60ml) olive oil
GARLIC ANCHOVY CRUMBS
1 tablespoon olive oil
6 anchovy fillets, drained, chopped finely
3 cloves garlic, crushed
1½ cups (105g) stale breadcrumbs
1 tablespoon finely grated lemon rind
⅓ cup finely chopped fresh flat-leaf parsley
½ cup (40g) finely grated romano cheese

1   Remove and discard tough outer leaves from artichokes. Trim stems so artichoke bases sit flat. Using a small teaspoon, remove and discard hairy chokes from centre of artichokes; rinse artichokes under cold water.
2   Pack artichokes tightly, upside down, into 4.5-litre (18-cup) slow cooker; pour in the water, stock and juice. Cook, covered, on low, 8 hours.
3   Make garlic anchovy crumbs before serving.
4   Remove artichokes with slotted spoon; drain well. Serve artichokes with olive oil and garlic anchovy crumbs for dipping.
garlic anchovy crumbs   Heat oil in large frying pan; cook anchovy and garlic, stirring, until anchovy softens. Add breadcrumbs and rind; cook, stirring, until crumbs are browned lightly and crisp. Transfer to medium bowl; cool. Stir in parsley and cheese; season to taste.

prep + cook time 8 hours 35 minutes
nutritional count per serving 6.2g total fat (1.8g saturated fat); 648kJ (155 cal); 13.9g carbohydrate; 9.5g protein; 2.3g fibre

• not suitable to freeze.

tips Artichoke leaves are pulled off the whole artichoke, one by one, and eaten by scraping against the teeth to extract the soft flesh at the base of each leaf. In this recipe we suggest dipping the leaves in a full-flavoured olive oil and the flavoured crumbs before eating. **serving suggestion** Serve artichokes with some crusty bread and a green or tomato salad to make a main meal.

lamb, harissa and chickpea casserole

serves 6

1.2kg (2½ pounds) boned lamb shoulder,
    chopped coarsely
¼ cup (35g) plain (all-purpose) flour
1 tablespoon olive oil
1 medium red onion (170g), sliced thinly
2 cloves garlic, crushed
2cm (¾ inch) piece fresh ginger (10g), grated
1 teaspoon ground allspice
1½ cups (375ml) beef stock
2 tablespoons harissa paste
2 x 5cm (2 inch) strips orange rind
800g (30 ounces) canned chickpeas
    (garbanzo beans), rinsed, drained
⅓ cup coarsely chopped fresh mint

1 Toss lamb in flour to coat; shake off excess.
Heat half the oil in large frying pan; cook lamb,
in batches, until browned. Transfer to 4.5-litre
(18-cup) slow cooker.
2 Heat remaining oil in same pan; cook onion,
garlic and ginger, stirring, until onion softens. Add
allspice; cook, stirring, until fragrant. Add ½ cup of
the stock; cook, stirring, until mixture boils.
3 Stir onion mixture into cooker with remaining
stock, harissa, rind and chickpeas. Cook, covered,
on low, 7 hours.
4 Season to taste; sprinkle casserole with mint.

prep + cook time 7 hours 35 minutes
nutritional count per serving 23.1g total fat
(9g saturated fat); 2019kJ (483 cal);
19.9g carbohydrate; 46.2g protein; 5.5g fibre

serving suggestion Serve casserole with rice pilaf,
steamed rice or couscous.

• suitable to freeze at the end of step 3.

veal and rosemary casserole

serves 6

.2kg (2½ pounds) boned veal shoulder,
  chopped coarsely
¼ cup (35g) plain (all-purpose) flour
  tablespoon olive oil
  medium brown onion (150g), chopped coarsely
2 cloves garlic, crushed
½ cup (125ml) dry red wine
2 medium carrots (240g), chopped coarsely
2 stalks celery (300g), trimmed, chopped coarsely
2 medium parsnips (500g), chopped coarsely
½ cups (625ml) beef stock
3 sprigs fresh rosemary

1 Toss veal in flour to coat, shake off excess.
Heat half the oil in large frying pan; cook veal,
n batches, until browned. Transfer to 4.5-litre
18-cup) slow cooker.

2 Heat remaining oil in same pan; cook onion
and garlic, stirring, until onion softens. Add wine;
bring to the boil. Boil, uncovered, until liquid
reduces by half.
3 Stir onion mixture into cooker with carrot, celery,
parsnip, stock and rosemary. Cook, covered, on
low, 8 hours. Season to taste.

prep + cook time 8 hours 35 minutes
nutritional count per serving 8.6g total fat
(2g saturated fat); 1513kJ (362 cal);
15.6g carbohydrate; 49.5g protein; 4.2g fibre

tip The butcher might have some good stewing
veal available, it's fine to use in this recipe.
serving suggestion Serve casserole with crusty
bread or soft creamy polenta.

• suitable to freeze at the end of step 3.

italian beef casserole

serves 6

1.2kg (2½ pounds) beef blade steak,
  chopped coarsely
¼ cup (35g) plain (all-purpose) flour
1 tablespoon olive oil
1 large brown onion (200g), chopped coarsely
2 cloves garlic, crushed
½ teaspoon dried chilli flakes
½ cup (125ml) dry red wine
400g (14½ ounces) canned diced tomatoes
¼ cup (70g) tomato paste
2½ cups (625ml) beef stock
2 dried bay leaves
1 large red capsicum (bell pepper) (350g),
  chopped coarsely
1 tablespoon finely chopped fresh oregano
⅓ cup coarsely chopped fresh basil
1 large zucchini (150g), halved lengthways,
  sliced thickly
185g (6 ounces) swiss brown mushrooms, halved
⅓ cup loosely packed fresh basil leaves

1 Toss beef in flour to coat, shake off excess. Heat half the oil in large frying pan; cook beef, in batches, until browned. Transfer to 4.5-litre (18-cup) slow cooker.

2 Heat remaining oil in same pan; cook onion, garlic and chilli, stirring, until onion softens. Add wine; bring to the boil. Boil, uncovered, until liquid reduces by half.

3 Stir onion mixture into cooker with undrained tomatoes, paste, stock, bay leaves, capsicum, oregano and the chopped basil. Cook, covered, on low, 8 hours.

4 Add zucchini and mushrooms to cooker for last 30 minutes of cooking time. Discard bay leaves. Season to taste.

5 Sprinkle casserole with basil leaves to serve.

prep + cook time 8 hours 30 minutes
nutritional count per serving 16.8g total fat (6.2g saturated fat); 1731kJ (414 cal); 12.5g carbohydrate; 47.6g protein; 4g fibre

• suitable to freeze at the end of step 3.

serving suggestion Serve casserole with creamy polenta, mashed potato or pasta.

seafood in romesco sauce

serves 6

1kg (2 pounds) cleaned whole baby octopus
800g (28 ounces) canned crushed tomatoes
4 cloves garlic, crushed
1 teaspoon dried chilli flakes
2 teaspoons smoked paprika
2 medium red capsicums (bell peppers) (400g),
  sliced thinly
2 tablespoons red wine vinegar
500g (1 pound) uncooked medium king prawns
  (shrimp)
500g (1 pound) cleaned mussels
½ cup (60g) ground almonds
½ cup coarsely chopped fresh flat-leaf parsley
⅓ cup coarsely chopped fresh oregano

1 Combine octopus, undrained tomatoes, garlic, chilli, paprika, capsicum and vinegar in 4.5-litre (18-cup) slow cooker; cook, covered, on low, 4 hours.
2 Meanwhile, shell and devein prawns, leaving tails intact. Add prawns, mussels and ground almonds to cooker; cook, covered, stirring occasionally, on high, about 20 minutes or until prawns change colour and mussels open (discard any that do not.)
3 Serve sprinkled with herbs.

prep + cook time 4 hours 45 minutes
nutritional count per serving 9.5g total fat (1.2g saturated fat); 1509kJ (361 cal); 9.5g carbohydrate; 57.1g protein; 3.7g fibre

tip Packets of ground almonds are sometimes sold as almond meal. They are available from health-food stores and most major supermarkets.
serving suggestion Serve with steamed rice or crusty bread.

• not suitable to freeze.

rabbit with sweet potato and sage

serves 6

1.5kg (3¼ pound) rabbit
12 baby brown onions (300g)
1 medium white sweet potato (450g),
  chopped coarsely
2 medium potatoes (400g), chopped coarsely
1 cup (250ml) verjuice
1 cup (250ml) chicken stock
2 cloves garlic, sliced thinly
¼ cup loosely packed fresh sage leaves

1   Cut rabbit into six serving-sized pieces. Peel
onions, leaving root ends intact.
2   Combine rabbit, onion and remaining ingredients
in 4.5-litre (18-cup) slow cooker; cook, covered, on
low, 6 hours. Season to taste.
3   Serve rabbit and vegetables drizzled with broth.

prep + cook time 6 hours 20 minutes
nutritional count per serving 4.6g total fat
(1.7g saturated fat); 1112kJ (266 cal);
21.6g carbohydrate; 32.6g protein; 3g fibre

tips Ask the butcher to cut the rabbit into pieces
for you.
Verjuice is available in delis and supermarkets; it's
usually found in the vinegar aisle. It's made from
unripe grapes and has a slightly acidic taste.
serving suggestion Serve with crusty bread and
steamed beans or broccoli.

• not suitable to freeze.

beef, date and spinach tagine

serves 6

1.2kg (2½ pounds) beef blade steak,
  chopped coarsely
¼ cup (35g) plain (all-purpose) flour
1 tablespoon olive oil
1 large red onion (300g), chopped finely
2 cloves garlic, crushed
1 teaspoon ground cinnamon
1 teaspoon ground cumin
½ teaspoon ground ginger
½ teaspoon ground turmeric
¼ teaspoon saffron threads
1 cup (250ml) beef stock
400g (14½ ounces) canned diced tomatoes
¾ cup (100g) seeded dried dates
315g (10 ounces) spinach, shredded coarsely
1 tablespoon thinly sliced preserved lemon rind
⅓ cup (45g) coarsely chopped roasted
  unsalted pistachios

1 Toss beef in flour to coat, shake off excess.
Heat half the oil in large frying pan; cook beef,
in batches, until browned. Transfer to 4.5-litre
(18-cup) slow cooker.
2 Heat remaining oil in same pan; cook onion
and garlic, stirring, until onion softens. Add spices;
cook, stirring, until fragrant. Add ½ cup of the
stock; cook, stirring, until mixture boils.
3 Transfer onion mixture to cooker with remaining
stock and undrained tomatoes; stir to combine.
Cook, covered, on low, 8 hours.
4 Add dates, spinach and half the preserved lemon
rind; cook, covered, on high, about 10 minutes or
until spinach wilts. Season to taste.
5 Sprinkle tagine with nuts and remaining preserved
lemon rind.

prep + cook time 8 hours 35 minutes
nutritional count per serving 20.4g total fat
(6.5g saturated fat); 1977kJ (473 cal);
22g carbohydrate; 47.5g protein; 5.6g fibre

• suitable to freeze at the end of step 3.

tips Beef shin or chuck steak could also be used.
Preserved lemon is available at delis and some supermarkets.
Remove and discard the lemon flesh, wash the rind, then use
it as the recipe directs.
serving suggestion Serve tagine with steamed couscous or rice.

best-ever bolognese sauce

serves 6

1 tablespoon olive oil
125g (4 ounce) piece prosciutto, chopped finely
2 medium brown onions (300g), chopped finely
1 large carrot (180g), chopped finely
2 stalks celery (300g), trimmed, chopped finely
2 cloves garlic, crushed
500g (1 pound) minced (ground) veal
500g (1 pound) minced (ground) pork
1 cup (250ml) dry red wine
1½ cups (375ml) beef stock
¼ cup (70g) tomato paste
1kg (2 pounds) ripe tomatoes, peeled, seeded, chopped coarsely
⅓ cup finely chopped fresh basil
2 tablespoons finely chopped fresh oregano

1 Heat half the oil in large frying pan; cook prosciutto, stirring, until crisp. Add onion, carrot, celery and garlic; cook, stirring, until vegetables soften. Transfer to 4.5-litre (18-cup) slow cooker.
2 Heat remaining oil in same pan; cook minces, stirring, until browned. Add wine; bring to the boil. Stir mince mixture into cooker with stock, paste and tomatoes; cook, covered, on low, 10 hours.
3 Stir in herbs; cook, covered, on high, 10 minutes. Season to taste.

prep + cook time 10 hours 40 minutes
nutritional count per serving 16.3g total fat (5.4g saturated fat); 1576kJ (377 cal); 7.4g carbohydrate; 41.7g protein; 3.5g fibre

tips Prosciutto can be replaced with bacon. Fresh tomatoes can be replaced with 800g (28 ounces) canned diced tomatoes.
serving suggestion Serve bolognese with spaghetti or your favourite pasta; top with shaved parmesan cheese.

• suitable to freeze at the end of step 2.

chicken cacciatore

serves 6

2 tablespoons olive oil
12 chicken drumsticks (1.8kg), skin removed
1 medium brown onion (150g), sliced thickly
3 cloves garlic, crushed
3 drained anchovy fillets, crushed
½ cup (125ml) dry white wine
⅓ cup (80ml) chicken stock
⅓ cup (80ml) tomato pasta sauce
2 tablespoons tomato paste
2 teaspoons finely chopped fresh basil
1 teaspoon caster (superfine) sugar
⅓ cup (55g) seeded black olives, halved
1 tablespoon finely chopped fresh flat-leaf parsley

1 Heat oil in large frying pan; cook chicken, in batches, until browned all over. Transfer chicken to 4.5-litre (18-cup) slow cooker.
2 Cook onion, garlic and anchovy in same pan, stirring, until onion softens. Add wine; bring to the boil. Boil, uncovered, until reduced by half; stir into cooker with stock, sauce, paste, basil and sugar. Cook, covered, on low, 6 hours.
3 Stir in olives and parsley; season to taste.

prep + cook time 6 hours 25 minutes
nutritional count per serving 18.5g total fat (4.4g saturated fat); 1501kJ (359 cal); 6.9g carbohydrate; 37.2g protein; 1.3g fibre

tip Use a plain (unflavoured) tomato-based sauce suitable for serving over pasta. These sauces can be bought in cans and jars and are often labelled "sugo" or "passata".
serving suggestion Serve cacciatore with creamy mashed potato or crusty bread.

• suitable to freeze at the end of step 2.

39

moroccan lamb with kumara and raisins

serves 6

2 tablespoons olive oil

1.2kg (2½ pounds) boned lamb shoulder, chopped coarsely

1 large brown onion (200g), sliced thickly

4 cloves garlic, crushed

2 tablespoons ras el hanout

2 cups (500ml) chicken stock

½ cup (125ml) water

1 tablespoon honey

2 medium kumara (orange sweet potato) (800g), chopped coarsely

400g (15 ounces) canned chickpeas (garbanzo beans), rinsed, drained

1 cinnamon stick

3 cardamom pods, bruised

⅓ cup (50g) raisins, halved

½ cup loosely packed fresh coriander (cilantro) leaves

⅓ cup (55g) coarsely chopped blanched almonds, roasted

1 Heat half the oil in large frying pan; cook lamb, in batches, until browned all over. Remove from pan. Heat remaining oil in same pan; cook onion and garlic, stirring, until onion is soft. Add ras el hanout; cook, stirring, until fragrant. Remove from heat; stir in stock, the water and honey.

2 Place kumara in 4.5-litre (18-cup) slow cooker; stir in chickpeas, cinnamon, cardamom, lamb and onion mixture. Cook, covered, on low, 6 hours. Season to taste.

3 Stir in raisins and coriander; sprinkle with nuts to serve.

prep + cook time 6 hours 25 minutes
nutritional count per serving 30.5g total fat (9.7g saturated fat); 2567kJ (614 cal); 34.9g carbohydrate; 47.2g protein; 6.3g fibre

• suitable to freeze at the end of step 2.

tip Ras el hanout is a blend of Moroccan spices available in delis and specialist food stores. If you can't find it, use a Moroccan seasoning available in supermarkets.

serving suggestion Serve tagine with buttered couscous and steamed baby green beans.

beef ribs with stout and caramelised onion

serves 6

1 tablespoon olive oil
2.5kg (5¼ pounds) racks beef short ribs
2 large brown onions (400g), sliced thinly
1 tablespoon light brown sugar
1 tablespoon balsamic vinegar
¼ cup (60ml) water
3 medium carrots (360g), sliced thickly
400g (14½ ounces) canned diced tomatoes
5 sprigs fresh thyme
1 tablespoon dijon mustard
1 cup (250ml) beef stock
1 cup (250ml) stout

1   Heat half the oil in large frying pan; cook ribs, in batches, until browned. Remove from pan.
2   Heat remaining oil in large frying pan; cook onion, stirring, until soft. Add sugar, vinegar and the water; cook, stirring occasionally, about 10 minutes or until onion caramelises.
3   Transfer onion mixture to 4.5-litre (18-cup) slow cooker; stir in carrot, undrained tomatoes, thyme, mustard, stock and stout. Add ribs, turn to coat in sauce mixture. Cook, covered, on low, 8 hours. Season to taste.
4   Cut ribs into serving-sized pieces; serve with the sauce.

prep + cook time 8 hours 45 minutes
nutritional count per serving 21.4g total fat (8.1g saturated fat); 2228kJ (533 cal); 12g carbohydrate; 67.2g protein; 3.5g fibre

tips For best results, get the butcher to cut the ribs into individual pieces. They become more tender and fit more easily into the slow cooker.
Stout is a strong-flavoured, dark-coloured type of beer originally from Britain. It is made with roasted barley, giving it its characteristic dark colour and bitter-sweet, almost coffee-like, flavour.
serving suggestion Serve ribs with steamed rice and a green leafy salad.

• suitable to freeze at the end of step 3.

chilli and brandy beef with white beans

serves 6

6 shallots (150g)
1.2kg (2½ pounds) beef brisket, chopped coarsely
1 fresh long red chilli, chopped finely
2 cloves garlic, crushed
3 medium egg (plum) tomatoes (225g),
 chopped coarsely
2 tablespoons tomato paste
1 cup (250ml) beef stock
¼ cup (60ml) brandy
400g (15 ounces) canned cannellini beans,
 rinsed, drained
⅓ cup coarsely chopped fresh flat-leaf parsley

1 Peel shallots, leaving root ends intact; cut
shallots in half lengthways.
2 Combine shallot, beef, chilli, garlic, tomato,
paste, stock and brandy in 4.5-litre (18-cup) slow
cooker; cook, covered, on low, 8 hours.
3 Add beans; cook, covered, on high, about
20 minutes or until hot. Stir in parsley; season
to taste.

prep + cook time 8 hours 25 minutes
nutritional count per serving 12.1g total fat
(5.1g saturated fat); 1375kJ (329 cal);
3.6g carbohydrate; 45g protein; 2.2g fibre

tips For a slightly richer colour and flavour, brown
the beef in a little oil in a frying pan before adding
it to the slow cooker.
Any type of white beans can be used; navy, great
northern or haricot are all good choices.
Beef brisket is an economical cut of meat; ask
the butcher to trim the fat away and to chop the
meat for you.
serving suggestion This recipe is quite hearty, a
simple green salad or crusty bread would go well
as an accompaniment.

• suitable to freeze at the end of step 2.

43

coq au vin

20 spring onions (500g)
2 tablespoons olive oil
6 rindless bacon slices (390g), sliced thinly
440g (14 ounces) button mushrooms
2 cloves garlic, crushed
1.8kg (3¾ pound) whole chicken
2 cups (500ml) dry red wine
2 medium carrots (240g), chopped coarsely
3 dried bay leaves
4 sprigs fresh thyme
2 sprigs fresh rosemary
1½ cups (375ml) chicken stock
¼ cup (70g) tomato paste
¼ cup (35g) cornflour (cornstarch)
2 tablespoons water

1 Trim green ends from onions, leaving about 4cm (1½ inches) of stem attached; trim roots leaving onions intact. Heat half the oil in large frying pan; cook onions, stirring, until browned all over, remove from pan. Add bacon, mushrooms and garlic to same pan; cook, stirring, until bacon is crisp, remove from pan.
2 Cut chicken into 12 pieces. Heat remaining oil in same pan; cook chicken, in batches, until browned all over; drain on absorbent paper. Add wine to same pan; bring to the boil, stirring.
3 Place chicken in 4.5-litre (18-cup) slow cooker with onions, bacon and mushroom mixture, carrot, herbs, stock, wine mixture and paste. Cook, covered, on low, 7 hours.
4 Stir in blended cornflour and the water; cook, covered, on high, about 20 minutes or until sauce thickens slightly. Season to taste.

prep + cook time 8 hours
nutritional count per serving 39.6g total fat (11.7g saturated fat); 2750kJ (658 cal); 12.3g carbohydrate; 47.8g protein; 5.1g fibre

• not suitable to freeze.

tips Use chicken pieces if you prefer, such as 6 thigh cutlets and 6 drumsticks or 6 marylands, or ask your butcher to cut the chicken into 12 serving pieces for you.
Use shallots instead of spring onions, if you like.
serving suggestion Serve coq au vin over creamy mashed potato drizzled with some of the sauce; accompany with a green salad.

pickled pork

3kg (6½ pound) hand of pickled pork
2 tablespoons brown malt vinegar
2 dried bay leaves
1 teaspoon black peppercorns
2 tablespoons dark brown sugar
1.5 litres (6 cups) water, approximately

1 Place pork, vinegar, bay leaves, peppercorns, and sugar in 4.5-litre (18-cup) slow cooker; add enough of the water to barely cover pork. Cook, covered, on low, 8 hours.
2 Carefully remove pork from cooking liquid; cover, stand 10 minutes before slicing. Discard cooking liquid.

prep + cook time 8 hours 10 minutes
nutritional count per serving 27.8g total fat (10.7g saturated fat); 2801kJ (670 cal); 4.2g carbohydrate; 100.7g protein; 0g fibre

tip The "hand" of pickled pork is a portion of leg and breast. You might need to order this from the butcher in advance.
serving suggestions Pickled pork is delicious served hot with mashed potato, wilted cabbage and mustard or it can be served cold (like ham) with potato salad or coleslaw.

• not suitable to freeze.

honey and balsamic braised pork

serves 6

2 tablespoons olive oil
1.2kg (2½ pound) piece pork neck
9 shallots (225g), halved
1½ cups (375ml) chicken stock
⅓ cup (80ml) white balsamic vinegar
¼ cup (90g) honey
6 cloves garlic, peeled
2 sprigs fresh rosemary
1 cup (160g) seeded green olives

1 Heat oil in large frying pan; cook pork until browned all over. Remove from pan.
2 Add shallots to same pan; cook, stirring, until browned all over. Add stock, vinegar and honey; bring to the boil.

3 Place garlic and rosemary in 4.5-litre (18-cup) slow cooker; top with pork. Pour over shallot mixture; cook, covered, on low, 7 hours.
4 Add olives; cook, covered, on low, 30 minutes. Season to taste.
5 Remove pork; stand, covered, 10 minutes before slicing. Serve pork drizzled with sauce.

prep + cook time 8 hours
nutritional count per serving 23.6g total fat (6.5g saturated fat); 1969kJ (471 cal); 20g carbohydrate; 44g protein; 1.1g fibre

serving suggestion Serve pork with mashed potatoes or soft creamy polenta, plus some wilted shredded cabbage.

• suitable to freeze at the end of step 3.

47

chinese chicken hot pot

serves 6

1.8kg (3¾ pound) whole chicken
1 litre (4 cups) water
1 litre (4 cups) chicken stock
2 cups (500ml) chinese cooking wine
½ cup (125ml) light soy sauce
⅓ cup (80ml) oyster sauce
⅓ cup (75g) firmly packed light brown sugar
4 cloves garlic, bruised
6cm (2¼ inch) piece fresh ginger (30g),
   sliced thinly
3 star anise
1 teaspoon five-spice powder
2 fresh long red chillies, halved lengthways
500g (1 pound) baby buk choy, chopped coarsely
⅓ cup coarsely chopped fresh coriander (cilantro)
1 fresh long red chilli, extra, sliced thinly

1 Rinse chicken under cold water; pat dry, inside and out, with absorbent paper. Combine the water, stock, cooking wine, sauces, sugar, garlic, ginger, spices and chilli in 4.5-litre (18-cup) slow cooker. Add chicken; cook, covered, on low, 8 hours.
2 Remove chicken; strain broth through fine sieve into large bowl. Discard solids. Cover chicken to keep warm. Return broth to cooker. Add buk choy to cooker; cook, covered, on high, about 5 minutes or until tender.
3 Cut chicken into 6 pieces; serve with buk choy, drizzle with the broth. Sprinkle with coriander and extra chilli.

prep + cook time 8 hours 20 minutes
nutritional count per serving 25.2g total fat
(7.9g saturated fat); 2077kJ (487 cal);
20.8g carbohydrate; 34.8g protein; 1.7g fibre

• suitable to freeze at the end of step 1.

tip Chinese cooking wine is also known as chinese rice wine and shao hsing wine. Dry sherry can be used instead.
serving suggestion Serve with steamed fresh rice noodles or rice.

creamy turkey stew with mustard

serves 8

4 turkey drumsticks (3kg), skin removed
2 tablespoons olive oil
375g (12 ounces) button mushrooms
2 medium leeks (700g), sliced thickly
4 rindless bacon slices (260g), chopped coarsely
2 cloves garlic, crushed
2 tablespoons plain (all-purpose) flour
1 cup (250ml) chicken stock
½ cup (125ml) dry white wine
2 tablespoons wholegrain (seedless) mustard
6 sprigs fresh lemon thyme
½ cup (125ml) pouring cream
2 teaspoons fresh lemon thyme leaves

1 Using sharp heavy knife, cut turkey meat from bones, chop meat coarsely; discard bones.
2 Heat oil in large frying pan; cook turkey, in batches, until browned all over. Transfer turkey to 4.5-litre (18-cup) slow cooker.

3 Add mushrooms, leek, bacon and garlic to same pan; cook, stirring, until leek softens. Add flour; cook, stirring, 1 minute. Stir in stock, wine, mustard and thyme sprigs; bring to the boil. Boil, uncovered, 2 minutes. Remove from heat; stir in cream. Transfer mushroom mixture to cooker. Cook, covered, on low, 2 hours.
4 Season to taste; sprinkle with thyme leaves.

prep + cook time 2 hours 30 minutes
nutritional count per serving 23.2g total fat (8.8g saturated fat); 1914kJ (458 cal); 5.3g carbohydrate; 53.2g protein; 3.1g fibre

tip Use 3kg turkey marylands if you can't get drumsticks.
serving suggestion Serve stew with mashed potato and steamed green beans.

• not suitable to freeze.

hungarian veal goulash

serves 6

1kg (2 pounds) boned veal shoulder,
  chopped coarsely
¼ cup (35g) plain (all-purpose) flour
1 tablespoon sweet paprika
2 teaspoons caraway seeds
½ teaspoon cayenne pepper
2 tablespoons olive oil
15g (½ ounce) butter
1 large brown onion (200g), chopped coarsely
2 cloves garlic, crushed
2 tablespoons tomato paste
1½ cups (375ml) beef stock
400g (14½ ounces) canned crushed tomatoes
3 small potatoes (360g), quartered
2 medium carrots (240g), chopped coarsely
½ cup (120g) sour cream
½ cup coarsely chopped fresh flat-leaf parsley

1   Toss veal in combined flour and spices to coat;
shake away excess flour. Heat half the oil and half
the butter in large frying pan; cook veal, in batches,
until browned all over. Transfer to 4.5-litre (18-cup)
slow cooker.
2   Heat remaining oil and butter in same pan; cook
onion and garlic, stirring, until onion is soft. Stir in
paste and stock; bring to the boil. Stir into cooker
with undrained tomatoes, potato and carrot; cook,
covered, on low, 8 hours.
3   Season to taste; dollop with sour cream and
sprinkle with parsley to serve.

prep + cook time 8 hours 30 minutes
nutritional count per serving 20.7g total fat
(8.7g saturated fat); 1835kJ (439 cal);
18.4g carbohydrate; 42.6g protein; 4.1g fibre

tip The butcher might have some good stewing
veal available; it's fine to use in this recipe.
serving suggestion Serve goulash with crusty
bread, rice or pasta.

• suitable to freeze at the end of step 2.

simple beef and vegetable casserole

serves 6

1.2kg (2½ pounds) beef chuck steak,
  chopped coarsely
⅓ cup (50g) plain (all-purpose) flour
¼ cup (60ml) olive oil
2 medium brown onions (300g), cut into
  thick wedges
2 medium carrots (240g), chopped coarsely
2 stalks celery (300g), trimmed, chopped coarsely
1 medium parsnip (250g), chopped coarsely
1 medium swede (rutabaga) (225g),
  chopped coarsely
3 cloves garlic, crushed
¼ cup (70g) tomato paste
400g (14½ ounces) canned crushed tomatoes
1 cup (250ml) beef stock
2 dried bay leaves
10 sprigs fresh thyme

1 Coat beef in flour; shake off excess. Heat
2 tablespoons of the oil in large frying pan; cook
beef, in batches, until browned all over. Transfer
beef to 4.5-litre (18-cup) slow cooker.
2 Heat remaining oil in same pan; cook onion,
carrot, celery, parsnip, swede and garlic; stirring,
until onion softens. Add paste; cook, stirring,
1 minute. Remove from heat; stir in undrained
tomatoes and stock.
3 Stir vegetable mixture and bay leaves into cooker;
add thyme. Cook, covered, on low, 8 hours. Discard
thyme and bay leaves; season to taste.

prep + cook time 8 hours 30 minutes
nutritional count per serving 18.7g total fat
(5.2g saturated fat); 1827kJ (437 cal);
19.3g carbohydrate; 44.9g protein; 5.9g fibre

• suitable to freeze at the end of step 3.

tips Use whatever vegetables you like: turnip, celeriac,
jerusalem artichokes are all good choices.
Gravy beef can be used instead of chuck steak.
Swede is also known as swedish turnip.
serving suggestion Serve casserole with crusty bread.

ratatouille

serves 6

2 tablespoons olive oil
1 large red onion (300g), chopped coarsely
3 cloves garlic, crushed
½ cup loosely packed fresh basil leaves
2 tablespoons tomato paste
3 cups (700g) bottled tomato pasta sauce
2 teaspoons caster (superfine) sugar
1 large eggplant (500g), chopped coarsely
2 medium red capsicum (bell pepper) (400g),
  chopped coarsely
2 large zucchini (300g), chopped coarsely
1 medium green capsicum (200g),
  chopped coarsely

1 Heat oil in large frying pan; cook onion, garlic
and half the basil, stirring, until onion softens. Add
paste; cook, stirring, 1 minute. Remove from heat,
stir in pasta sauce and sugar.

2 Place vegetables and sauce mixture into 4.5-litre
(18-cup) slow cooker. Cook, covered, on low, 4 hours.
Season to taste.
3 Serve ratatouille sprinkled with remaining basil.

prep + cook time 4 hours 20 minutes
nutritional count per serving 7.5g total fat
(1g saturated fat); 803kJ (192 cal);
22.1g carbohydrate; 5.5g protein; 7g fibre

tip Use a plain (unflavoured) tomato-based sauce
suitable for serving over pasta. These sauces can
be bought in cans and jars and are often labelled
"sugo" or "passata".
serving suggestion Serve ratatouille with soft
creamy polenta.

• suitable to freeze at the end of step 2, although
it's much better eaten straight after cooking.

veal with parsley and capers

serves 6

1.2kg (2½ pounds) boned veal shoulder,
  chopped coarsely
⅓ cup (50g) plain (all-purpose) flour
¼ cup (60ml) olive oil
8 shallots (200g)
375g (12 ounces) button mushrooms
1 cup (250ml) dry white wine
4 bacon bones (320g)
1 cup (250ml) chicken stock
4 dried bay leaves
1 cup (120g) frozen peas, thawed
1 cup coarsely chopped fresh flat-leaf parsley
1 tablespoon rinsed, drained baby capers
2 teaspoons finely grated lemon rind
2 cloves garlic, chopped finely

1   Coat veal in flour; shake off excess. Heat 2 tablespoons of the oil in large frying pan; cook veal, in batches, until browned all over. Transfer veal to 4.5-litre (18-cup) slow cooker.
2   Meanwhile, peel shallots, leave roots intact. Heat remaining oil in same pan; cook shallots and mushrooms, stirring, until browned. Add wine, bring to the boil; boil, uncovered, until reduced by half.
3   Add bacon bones, stock, bay leaves and shallot mixture to cooker. Cook, covered, on low, 6 hours.
4   Discard bacon bones and bay leaves. Stir in peas, parsley, capers, rind and garlic; season to taste.

prep + cook time 6 hours 30 minutes
nutritional count per serving 16.5g total fat (3.4g saturated fat); 1814kJ (434 cal); 9.1g carbohydrate; 53.4g protein; 4g fibre

tip The butcher might have some good stewing veal available, it's fine to use in this recipe.
serving suggestion Serve with creamy mashed potato and a green leafy salad.

• not suitable to freeze.

55

osso buco with mixed mushrooms

serves 6

6 large pieces beef osso buco (1.7kg)
¼ cup (35g) plain (all-purpose) flour
2 tablespoons olive oil
1 large brown onion (200g), chopped coarsely
1 cup (250ml) marsala
1½ cups (375ml) beef stock
¼ cup (60ml) worcestershire sauce
2 tablespoons wholegrain mustard
2 sprigs fresh rosemary
185g (6 ounces) swiss brown mushrooms,
  sliced thickly
155g (5 ounces) portabello mushrooms,
  cut into 8 wedges
155g (5 ounces) oyster mushrooms,
  chopped coarsely
½ cup (125ml) pouring cream
¼ cup (35g) gravy powder
2 tablespoons water
½ cup coarsely chopped fresh flat-leaf parsley

1 Coat beef all over in flour, shake off excess. Heat half the oil in large frying pan; cook beef, in batches, until browned all over. Remove from pan.
2 Heat remaining oil in same pan; cook onion, stirring, until onion softens. Add marsala; bring to the boil. Add onion mixture to 4.5-litre (18-cup) slow cooker; stir in stock, sauce, mustard and rosemary. Place beef in cooker, fitting pieces upright and tightly packed in a single layer. Add mushrooms to cooker. Cook, covered, on low, 8 hours.
3 Carefully remove beef from cooker; cover to keep warm. Add cream and combined gravy powder and the water to cooker; cook, covered, on high, 10 minutes or until mixture thickens slightly. Stir in parsley; season to taste.
4 Serve beef with mushroom sauce.

prep + cook time 8 hours 50 minutes
nutritional count per serving 16.5g total fat (7.1g saturated fat); 1902kJ (455 cal); 17.4g carbohydrate; 45.5g protein; 3.7g fibre

• not suitable to freeze.

tips Ask the butcher for either veal or beef shin (osso buco) – veal will be smaller than beef, in which case you will need about 12 pieces to serve six people.
You can use a mixture of mushrooms as we have, or just one variety with a good robust flavour – you need a total of 500g (1 pound).
serving suggestion Serve osso buco with a mash – potato, celeriac or kumara are all good – and a green leafy salad.

red wine, beef and mushroom stew

serves 6

16 spring onions (400g)
2 tablespoons olive oil
375g (12 ounces) button mushrooms
4 rindless bacon slices (260g), chopped coarsely
3 cloves garlic, crushed
1 cup (250ml) dry red wine
¼ cup (70g) tomato paste
½ teaspoon caster (superfine) sugar
1.2kg (2½ pounds) gravy beef, chopped coarsely
2 medium fennel bulbs (600g), sliced thickly
⅓ cup coarsely chopped fresh flat-leaf parsley

1 Trim green ends from onions, leaving about 8cm (3 inches) of stems attached; trim roots. Heat oil in large frying pan; cook onions, mushrooms, bacon and garlic, stirring, until onion softens. Stir in wine, paste and sugar; bring to the boil, boil, uncovered, 2 minutes.
2 Place beef, fennel and onion mixture in 4.5-litre (18-cup) slow cooker. Cook, covered, on low, 8 hours.
3 Stir in parsley; season to taste.

prep + cook time 8 hours 25 minutes
nutritional count per serving 21.3g total fat (6.8g saturated fat); 1952kJ (467 cal); 6.3g carbohydrate; 53.1g protein; 5.2g fibre

tip Chuck steak or any stewing steak can be used instead of gravy beef.
serving suggestion Serve stew over creamy polenta or mashed potato; accompany with steamed green beans.

• not suitable to freeze.

creamy potato bake

serves 8 [as an accompaniment]

1 tablespoon olive oil
2 medium leeks (700g), sliced thinly
4 rindless bacon slices (260g), chopped finely
2 tablespoons coarsely chopped fresh
  flat-leaf parsley
1.5kg (3¼ pounds) potatoes, sliced thinly
2 cups (500ml) pouring cream
¼ cup (60ml) milk
1 tablespoon dijon mustard
50g packet dried chicken noodle soup mix
½ cup (60g) coarsely grated cheddar cheese
½ cup (40g) finely grated parmesan cheese

1 Heat oil in large frying pan; cook leek and
bacon, stirring, until leek softens. Remove from
heat; stir in parsley.
2 Layer one third of the potato in 4.5-litre (18-cup)
slow cooker; top with half the leek mixture. Repeat
layering with remaining potato and leek, finishing
with potato layer.
3 Combine cream, milk, mustard and soup mix
in large jug, pour over potatoes; sprinkle with
combined cheeses. Cook, covered, on low, 6 hours.

prep + cook time 6 hours 25 minutes
nutritional count per serving 38.7g total fat
(22.7g saturated fat); 2257kJ (540 cal);
29.5g carbohydrate; 17.3g protein; 4.3g fibre

tip It's important to slice the potatoes thinly; a
mandolin or V-slicer makes the job quick and easy.
serving suggestion Serve spoonfuls of the bake
with a green leafy salad as a light meal, or serve
the bake as an accompaniment to a main course.

• not suitable to freeze.

braised beef cheeks in stout

serves 6

2 tablespoons olive oil
6 beef cheeks (1.5kg)
12 shallots (300g)
2 cloves garlic, crushed
1 cup (250ml) beef stock
2 medium carrots (240g), chopped coarsely
250g portabello mushrooms, chopped coarsely
3 cups (750ml) stout
2 tablespoons dark brown sugar
2 sprigs fresh rosemary
¼ cup (35g) cornflour (cornstarch)
2 tablespoons water

1 Heat half the oil in large frying pan; cook beef, in batches, until browned all over. Transfer to 4.5-litre (18-cup) slow cooker.
2 Meanwhile, peel shallots, trim roots, leaving shallots whole; halve shallots lengthways.
3 Heat remaining oil in same pan; cook shallots and garlic, stirring, until shallots are browned lightly. Add stock; bring to the boil. Stir shallot mixture into cooker with carrot, mushrooms, stout, sugar and rosemary. Cook, covered, on low, 9 hours.
4 Carefully remove beef from cooker; cover to keep warm. Stir blended cornflour and the water into cooker; cook, covered, on high, about 15 minutes or until thickened slightly. Season to taste.
5 Serve beef with sauce.

prep + cook time 9 hours 45 minutes
nutritional count per serving 26.2g total fat (9.4g saturated fat); 2424kJ (580 cal); 16.8g carbohydrate; 55.7g protein; 2.8g fibre

• not suitable to freeze.

tips Beef cheeks are available from most butchers, but you might need to order them in advance. Substitute beef shin, chuck or blade steak if cheeks are unavailable.
Stout is a strong-flavoured, dark-coloured beer made from barley.
serving suggestion Serve beef with creamy mashed potato or colcannon (mashed potatoes with cabbage).

honey soy lamb chops

serves 6

¼ cup (60ml) salt-reduced soy sauce
¼ cup (90g) honey
3 cloves garlic, crushed
1 teaspoon sesame oil
2 large red onions (600g), cut into thick wedges
6 lamb forequarter chops (1.2kg)
6 sprigs fresh rosemary
15g (½ ounce) butter, melted
1 tablespoon plain (all-purpose) flour

1 Combine sauce, honey, garlic and oil in small jug.
2 Place onion in 4.5-litre (18-cup) slow cooker; top with lamb, soy sauce mixture and rosemary. Cook, covered, on low, 6 hours.
3 Discard rosemary, remove lamb from cooker; cover to keep warm.

4 Combine butter and flour in small bowl; stir into cooker. Cook, covered, on high, about 25 minutes or until sauce thickens; season to taste. Strain sauce through fine sieve into medium heatproof jug; discard onion.
5 Serve lamb drizzled with sauce.

prep + cook time 6 houtes
nutritional count per serving 16.9g total fat (8.2g saturated fat); 1588kJ (380cal); 19.5g carbohydrate; 36.2g protein; 1.6g fibre

serving suggestion Steamed kipfler potatoes, baby peas and carrots make a great accompaniment.

• suitable to freeze at the end of step 2.

lamb and potato stew with spinach

serves 6

3 medium potatoes (600g), unpeeled, cut into thick wedges
2 large brown onions (400g), sliced thickly
2 large carrots (360g), sliced thickly
4 cloves garlic, sliced thinly
1.2kg (2½ pounds) boned lamb leg, chopped coarsely
1½ cups (375ml) chicken stock
1⅔ cups (410g) canned tomato puree
4 sprigs fresh thyme
60g (2 ounces) baby spinach leaves

1 Place potatoes, onion, carrot, garlic and lamb in 4.5-litre (18-cup) slow cooker; stir in stock, puree and thyme. Cook, covered, on low, 6 hours.
2 Discard thyme. Stir in spinach leaves; season to taste.

prep + cook time 6 hours 20 minutes
nutritional count per serving 11.4g total fat (4.9g saturated fat); 1676kJ (401 cal); 21.6g carbohydrate; 49.6g protein; 5.9g fibre

serving suggestion Serve stew with crusty bread and steamed green vegetables.

• not suitable to freeze.

chilli beans with tomato sauce

serves 6

1 tablespoon olive oil
6 rindless bacon slices (390g), chopped finely
1 stalk celery (150g), trimmed, chopped finely
1 small brown onion (80g), chopped finely
1 small carrot (70g), chopped finely
1 fresh long red chilli, chopped finely
¼ cup (70g) tomato paste
3 cups (700g) bottled tomato pasta sauce
¾ cup (180ml) chicken stock
2 teaspoons caster (superfine) sugar
800g (30 ounces) canned cannellini beans,
  rinsed, drained
¼ cup coarsely chopped fresh flat-leaf parsley

1 Heat oil in medium frying pan; cook bacon, celery, onion, carrot and chilli, stirring, until onion softens. Add paste; cook, stirring, 1 minute. Transfer mixture to 4.5-litre (18-cup) slow cooker. Stir in sauce, stock, sugar and beans. Cook, covered, on low, 8 hours.
2 Stir in parsley; season to taste.

prep + cook time 8 hours 30 minutes
nutritional count per serving 12.9g total fat
(3.9g saturated fat); 1112kJ (266 cal);
17.8g carbohydrate; 17.3g protein; 5.2g fibre

• suitable to freeze at the end of step 1.

tips Instead of the cannellini beans, you can use any canned white beans you like, such as great northern, navy or haricot.
Use a plain (unflavoured) tomato-based sauce suitable for serving over pasta. These sauces can be bought in cans and jars and are often labelled "sugo" or "passata".
serving suggestion Serve with toasted sourdough or cornbread.

chorizo, chilli and bean stew

serves 6

1 tablespoon olive oil
1 large red onion (300g), chopped coarsely
3 chorizo sausages (500g), chopped coarsely
4 cloves garlic, crushed
1 teaspoon dried chilli flakes
1 medium red capsicum (bell pepper) (200g),
  chopped coarsely
150g baby green beans, halved
800g (30 ounces) canned cannellini beans,
  rinsed, drained
800g (28 ounces) canned diced tomatoes
⅓ cup (80ml) chicken stock
2 dried bay leaves
⅓ cup coarsely chopped fresh flat-leaf parsley

1 Heat oil in large frying pan; cook onion and
chorizo, stirring, until browned lightly. Add garlic
and chilli flakes; cook, stirring, until fragrant.
2 Combine capsicum, both beans, undrained
tomatoes, stock, bay leaves and chorizo mixture
in 4.5-litre (18-cup) slow cooker. Cook, covered,
on low, 3 hours.
3 Discard bay leaves. Season to taste; sprinkle
with parsley.

prep + cook time 3 hours 20 minutes
nutritional count per serving 28.7g total fat
(9.6g saturated fat); 1689kJ (404 cal);
13.1g carbohydrate; 21.3g protein; 5.8g fibre

serving suggestion Serve stew with a green salad
and some crusty bread.

• suitable to freeze at the end of step 2.

tomato tripe stew with pancetta

serves 6

1.5kg (3¼ pounds) honeycomb tripe
1 tablespoon olive oil
1 medium brown onion (150g), chopped coarsely
2 cloves garlic, crushed
6 slices pancetta (90g), chopped coarsely
⅓ cup (80ml) dry white wine
1 large carrot (180g), chopped coarsely
1 stalk celery (150g), trimmed, chopped coarsely
3 cups (700g) bottled tomato pasta sauce
2 dried bay leaves
½ cup coarsely chopped fresh flat-leaf parsley

1 Cover tripe with cold water in large saucepan; bring to the boil. Boil, covered, 10 minutes. Drain. Cut tripe into 4cm (1½ inch) pieces, transfer to 4.5-litre (18-cup) slow cooker.
2 Meanwhile, heat oil in small frying pan; cook onion, garlic and pancetta, stirring, until onion softens and pancetta is browned and crisp.
3 Transfer onion mixture to cooker; stir in wine, carrot, celery, sauce and bay leaves. Cook, covered, on low, 6 hours.
4 Discard bay leaves. Season to taste. Sprinkle stew with parsley.

prep + cook time 6 hours 30 minutes
nutritional count per serving 11.3g total fat (3.6g saturated fat); 1371kJ (328 cal); 14g carbohydrate; 38.3g protein; 3.9g fibre

tips Check with the butcher to make sure the tripe has been cleaned and blanched. We suggest you blanch the tripe again – see step 1 – before cutting it into pieces. You might have to order the tripe from the butcher in advance.
Use a plain (unflavoured) tomato-based sauce suitable for serving over pasta. These sauces can be bought in cans and jars and are often labelled "sugo" or "passata".
serving suggestion Serve stew with crusty bread.

• not suitable to freeze.

lamb tagine with harissa and green olives

serves 6

1.2kg (2½ pounds) boned lamb shoulder, chopped coarsely
1 large red onion (300g), grated coarsely
2 cloves garlic, crushed
2 tablespoons finely chopped coriander (cilantro) root and stem mixture
1 cinnamon stick, halved
1 teaspoon ground cumin
1 teaspoon ground ginger
1 teaspoon sweet paprika
⅓ cup (80ml) olive oil
1 tablespoon harissa
800g (28 ounces) canned diced tomatoes
¼ cup (70g) tomato paste
½ cup (125ml) beef stock
400g (15 ounces) canned chickpeas (garbanzo beans), rinsed, drained
2 tablespoons honey
½ cup (90g) seeded small green olives
2 teaspoons finely chopped preserved lemon rind
½ cup loosely packed fresh mint leaves

1 Combine lamb, onion, garlic, coriander root and stem mixture, spices and half the oil in large bowl.
2 Heat remaining oil in large frying pan; cook lamb, in batches, until browned all over. Transfer lamb to 4.5-litre (18-cup) slow cooker.
3 Stir harissa, undrained tomatoes, paste, stock, chickpeas and honey into cooker. Cook, covered, on low, 4 hours.
4 Remove cinnamon stick; stir in olives and lemon rind. Season to taste; sprinkle with mint.

prep + cook time 4 hours 35 minutes
nutritional count per serving 32g total fat (10.2g saturated fat); 2424kJ (580 cal); 26.3g carbohydrate; 44.1g protein; 5.7g fibre

• suitable to freeze at the end of step 3.

tips The lamb mixture can be marinaded overnight at the end of step 1. Preserved lemon is available at delis and some supermarkets. Remove and discard the flesh, wash the rind, then use it as the recipe directs. serving suggestion Serve with couscous flavoured with chopped preserved lemon rind and coarsely chopped fresh mint leaves.

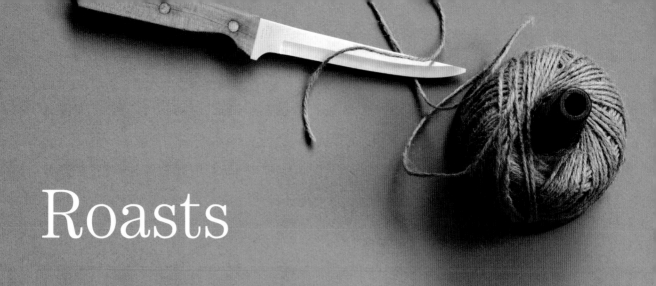

Roasts

chicken with leeks and artichokes serves 4

1.6kg (3¼ pound) whole chicken
1 unpeeled lemon, chopped coarsely
4 cloves unpeeled garlic
4 sprigs fresh tarragon
6 sprigs fresh flat-leaf parsley
45g (1½ ounces) butter
¾ cup (180ml) dry white wine
2 medium globe artichokes (400g), quartered
8 baby leeks (640g)
1 cup (250ml) chicken stock

1 Wash chicken under cold water; pat dry inside and out with absorbent paper. Place lemon, garlic and herbs in chicken cavity; season with salt and pepper. Tuck wing tips under; tie legs together with kitchen string.
2 Melt butter in large frying pan; cook chicken until browned all over. Remove chicken. Add wine; bring to the boil.
3 Meanwhile, trim stems from artichokes; remove tough outer leaves. Place artichokes and leeks in 4.5-litre (18-cup) slow cooker; add wine mixture and stock. Place chicken on vegetables; cook, covered, on low, 6 hours.
4 Serve chicken with vegetables; drizzle with a little of the juice.

prep + cook time 6 hours 30 minutes
nutritional count per serving 42.2g total fat (16.3g saturated fat); 2571kJ (615 cal); 5.6g carbohydrate; 44.9g protein; 4.2g fibre

tip Replace the baby leeks with 1 large leek (500g), sliced thickly.
serving suggestion Serve chicken with creamy mashed potatoes and a green leafy salad.

• not suitable to freeze.

green olive and lemon chicken

serves 4

15g (½ ounce) butter, softened
1 tablespoon olive oil
2 teaspoons finely grated lemon rind
3 cloves garlic, crushed
¼ cup (30g) seeded green olives, chopped finely
2 tablespoons finely chopped fresh flat-leaf parsley
1.5kg (3¼ pound) whole chicken
2 unpeeled medium lemons (280g), quartered

prep + cook time 6 hours 20 minutes
nutritional count per serving 38.1g total fat
(12.1g saturated fat); 2086kJ (499 cal);
2g carbohydrate; 37.7g protein; 0.6g fibre

tip Kitchen string is made of a natural product such as cotton or hemp so that it neither affects the flavour of the food it's tied around nor melts when heated.
serving suggestion Serve with roasted potatoes and steamed green vegetables, or creamy polenta or mash and a green salad.

• not suitable to freeze.

1 Combine butter, oil, rind, garlic, olives and parsley in medium bowl; season.
2 Rinse chicken under cold water; pat dry, inside and out, with absorbent paper. Use fingers to make a pocket between the breasts and skin; push half the butter mixture under skin. Rub remaining butter mixture all over chicken. Tuck wing tips under; fill cavity with lemon, tie legs together with kitchen string. Trim skin around neck; secure neck flap to underside of chicken with small fine skewers.
3 Place chicken in 4.5-litre (18-cup) slow cooker. Cook, covered, on low, 6 hours.
4 Cut chicken into quarters to serve.

pork neck with cider and pear

serves 4

1kg (2 pound) piece pork neck
185g (6 ounces) italian pork sausages
1 egg yolk
½ cup (70g) coarsely chopped pistachios
2 tablespoons coarsely chopped fresh sage
1 tablespoon olive oil
1 medium brown onion (150g), quartered
4 cloves garlic, halved
2 medium unpeeled pears (460g), quartered
⅔ cup (160ml) alcoholic apple cider
6 fresh sage leaves

1 Place pork on board; slice through thickest part of pork horizontally, without cutting all the way through. Open pork out to form one large piece; trim pork.
2 Squeeze filling from sausages into small bowl, mix in egg yolk, nuts and chopped sage; season. Press sausage mixture along one long side of pork; roll pork to enclose filling. Tie pork with kitchen string at 2.5cm (1 inch) intervals.

3 Heat oil in large frying pan; cook pork until browned all over. Remove from pan. Add onion and garlic to same pan; cook, stirring, until onion softens.
4 Place pears and onion mixture in 4.5-litre (18-cup) slow cooker; top with pork then add cider and sage leaves. Cook, covered, on low, 6 hours.
5 Serve sliced pork with pear and onion mixture. Sprinkle with extra sage leaves, if you like.

prep + cook time 6 hours 30 minutes
nutritional count per serving 45.3g total fat (13g saturated fat); 3164kJ (757 cal); 19g carbohydrate; 63g protein; 5.6g fibre

tip Italian sausages are coarse pork sausages generally sold in plump links. They are usually flavoured with garlic and fennel seed or anise seed, and come in two styles – hot (flavoured with thai red chilli) and sweet (without the added heat). They are available from speciality butchers and delicatessens.
serving suggestion Serve pork with creamy mashed potato and a radicchio or witlof salad.

• not suitable to freeze.

73

beef pot roast

serves 4

¼ cup (60ml) olive oil
4 small potatoes (180g), unpeeled, halved
375g (12 ounce) piece unpeeled pumpkin, cut into
  4 wedges
8 baby onions (200g), halved
375g (12 ounces) baby carrots
250g (8 ounces) jerusalem artichokes (sunchokes)
750g (1½ pound) piece beef blade steak
1 tablespoon wholegrain mustard
2 teaspoons smoked paprika
2 teaspoons finely chopped fresh rosemary
1 clove garlic, crushed
1½ cups (375ml) beef stock
½ cup (125ml) dry red wine
2 tablespoons balsamic vinegar
¼ cup (35g) gravy powder
2 tablespoons water

1 Heat 2 tablespoons of the oil in large frying pan; cook potato, pumpkin and onion, in batches, until browned all over. Place vegetables in 4.5-litre (18-cup) slow cooker with carrots and artichokes.
2 Heat 2 teaspoons of the remaining oil in same pan; cook beef until browned all over. Remove beef from pan; spread with combined mustard, paprika, rosemary, garlic and remaining oil.
3 Place beef on vegetables in slow cooker; pour over combined stock, wine and vinegar. Cook, covered, on low, 8 hours.
4 Remove beef and vegetables from cooker; cover beef, stand 10 minutes before slicing thinly. Cover vegetables to keep warm.
5 Meanwhile, blend gravy powder with the water in small bowl until smooth. Stir gravy mixture into liquid in slow cooker; cook, covered, on high, about 10 minutes or until gravy is thickened slightly. Season to taste. Strain gravy.
6 Serve beef with gravy and vegetables.

prep + cook time 8 hours 30 minutes
nutritional count per serving 26.8g total fat
(7.5g saturated fat); 2353kJ (563 cal);
25g carbohydrate; 46.8g protein; 7.1g fibre

• not suitable to freeze.

tips We used nicola potatoes and jap pumpkin in this recipe. Jerusalem artichokes can be hard to find. You can leave them out and add swede, parsnip or turnip to the pot roast instead. Gravy powder is an instant gravy mix made with browned flour. Plain (all-purpose) flour can be used for thickening instead.
serving suggestion Serve with steamed green beans or broccoli.

mexican slow-roasted lamb shanks

serves 4

2 medium tomatoes (300g), chopped coarsely
1 medium red capsicum (bell pepper) (200g), chopped coarsely
1 medium yellow capsicum (bell pepper) (200g), chopped coarsely
2 tablespoons olive oil
2 teaspoons sweet paprika
2 teaspoons ground cumin
1 teaspoon ground coriander
2 cloves garlic, crushed
1 fresh long red chilli, chopped finely
2 tablespoons finely chopped fresh oregano
8 french-trimmed lamb shanks (2kg)

1 Combine tomato and capsicum in 4.5-litre (18-cup) slow cooker.
2 Combine oil, spices, garlic, chilli and oregano in large bowl; add lamb, turn to coat in marinade. Cook lamb in heated large frying pan, in batches, until browned. Transfer to cooker. Cook, covered, on low, 8 hours. Season to taste.
3 Serve lamb shanks drizzled with sauce; sprinkle with extra oregano leaves.

prep + cook time 8 hours 30 minutes
nutritional count per serving 14.1g total fat (3.5g saturated fat); 1659kJ (397 cal); 4.2g carbohydrate; 61.9g protein; 2g fibre

tip Lamb can be marinated in the spice mixture overnight, if you like.
serving suggestion Serve lamb with flour tortillas, lime wedges and a green salad.

• suitable to freeze at the end of step 2.

portuguese-style chicken

serves 4

¼ cup (60ml) olive oil
¼ cup (70g) tomato paste
4 cloves garlic, quartered
2 tablespoons finely grated lemon rind
⅓ cup (80ml) lemon juice
4 fresh small red thai (serrano) chillies,
  chopped coarsely
1 tablespoon smoked paprika
½ cup firmly packed fresh oregano leaves
1.8kg (3¾ pound) whole chicken
1 medium unpeeled lemon (140g), quartered
3 sprigs fresh lemon thyme

1 Blend or process 2 tablespoons of the oil, paste, garlic, rind, juice, chilli, paprika and oregano until smooth. Season to taste.
2 Rinse chicken under cold water; pat dry inside and out with absorbent paper. Place lemon quarters and thyme inside cavity of chicken; secure cavity with a fine skewer.

3 Make a pocket under skin of breast, drumsticks and thighs with fingers. Using disposable gloves, rub ¼ cup of paste under skin. Tuck wing tips under; tie legs together with kitchen string. Rub ¼ cup of paste all over chicken.
4 Heat remaining oil in large frying pan; cook chicken until browned all over. Transfer to 4.5-litre (18-cup) slow cooker. Cook, covered, on low, 6 hours.
5 Cut chicken into pieces; accompany with the remaining paste.

prep + cook time 6 hours 45 minutes
nutritional count per serving 50g total fat
(13.2g saturated fat); 2688kJ (643 cal);
2.9g carbohydrate; 45.8g protein; 1.5g fibre

tip Fresh chillies can burn your fingers, so wear disposable gloves when handling them.
serving suggestion Serve chicken with potato chips or wedges, a green salad and lemon wedges.

• not suitable to freeze.

slow-roasted chilli and fennel pork

serves 6

1kg (2 pound) piece pork shoulder on the bone, rind on
1 medium lemon (140g)
1½ tablespoons fennel seeds
2 teaspoons dried chilli flakes
2 teaspoons sea salt
½ teaspoon cracked black pepper
3 cloves garlic, chopped coarsely
⅓ cup (80ml) olive oil
1 large brown onion (200g), chopped coarsely
½ cup (125ml) chicken stock

1 Using a sharp knife, score pork rind in a criss-cross pattern. Coarsely grate rind from lemon; chop lemon coarsely.
2 Cook fennel seeds in dry large frying pan until fragrant. Using mortar and pestle, crush seeds. Add chilli, salt, pepper, garlic, lemon rind and 2 tablespoons of the oil; pound until ground finely.
3 Heat remaining oil in same pan; cook pork, skin-side down, until browned and crisp. Turn pork; cook until browned all over. Spread fennel mixture all over pork. Place onion, stock and chopped lemon in 4.5-litre (18-cup) slow cooker; top with pork, skin-side up. Cook, covered, on low, 7 hours.
4 Remove pork from cooker; stand, covered, 10 minutes before slicing thinly.

prep + cook time 7 hours 30 minutes
nutritional count per serving 24.3g total fat
(6.4g saturated fat); 1384kJ (331 cal);
2.1g carbohydrate; 26.1g protein; 0.7g fibre

• not suitable to freeze.

tip Ask the butcher to score the rind on the pork for you.
serving suggestion Serve sliced pork with your favourite chutney or relish in crusty bread rolls or baguettes with a green salad.

char siu pork ribs

serves 6

2.5kg (5¼ pounds) american-style pork spare ribs
2 tablespoons peanut oil
½ cup (125ml) char siu sauce
2 tablespoons light soy sauce
¼ cup (60ml) orange juice
5cm (2 inch) piece fresh ginger (25g), grated
2 cloves garlic, crushed
1 fresh long red chilli, chopped finely
2 teaspoons sesame oil

1   Cut rib racks into pieces to fit 4.5-litre (18-cup) slow cooker. Heat peanut oil in large frying pan; cook ribs, in batches, until browned all over.
2   Meanwhile, combine sauces, juice, ginger, garlic, chilli and sesame oil in jug; brush all over ribs. Place ribs in cooker; pour over remaining sauce. Cook, covered, on low, 7 hours.
3   Remove ribs from sauce; cover to keep warm. Place sauce in medium saucepan; bring to the boil. Boil, uncovered, about 5 minutes or until sauce is thickened slightly.
4   Serve ribs drizzled with sauce.

prep + cook time 7 hours 25 minutes
nutritional count per serving 23.9g total fat (6.6g saturated fat); 1760kJ (421 cal); 9.6g carbohydrate; 40.7g protein; 2.7g fibre

tip Ask the butcher to cut the rib racks into pieces that will fit your slow cooker.
serving suggestion Serve ribs with steamed rice and stir-fried asian greens.

• not suitable to freeze.

greek-style roast lamb with potatoes

serves 4

2 tablespoons olive oil
1kg (2 pounds) baby new potatoes
2kg (4 pound) lamb leg
2 sprigs fresh rosemary, chopped coarsely
2 tablespoons finely chopped fresh flat-leaf parsley
2 tablespoons finely chopped fresh oregano
3 cloves garlic, crushed
1 tablespoon finely grated lemon rind
2 tablespoons lemon juice
½ cup (125ml) beef stock

1 Heat half the oil in large frying pan; cook potatoes until browned. Transfer to 4.5-litre (18-cup) slow cooker.
2 Make small cuts in lamb at 2.5cm (1 inch) intervals; press rosemary into cuts. Combine remaining oil, parsley, oregano, garlic, rind and juice in small bowl; rub mixture all over lamb, season.

3 Cook lamb in same heated pan until browned all over. Place lamb on top of potatoes; add stock. Cook, covered, on low, 8 hours.
4 Remove lamb and potatoes; cover lamb, stand 10 minutes before slicing.
5 Serve lamb with potatoes and sauce.

prep + cook time 8 hours 40 minutes
nutritional count per serving 29.5g total fat (10.2g saturated fat); 3206kJ (767 cal); 33.5g carbohydrate; 88.4g protein; 5.6g fibre

serving suggestion Serve lamb with a greek salad or steamed spinach.

• not suitable to freeze. Lamb can be covered and refrigerated overnight at step 2.

lamb with quince and honey

serves 4

1kg (2 pound) piece boneless lamb shoulder
6 cloves garlic, peeled, halved
2 tablespoons finely chopped coriander (cilantro)
   root and stem mixture
2 teaspoons ground cumin
1 teaspoon ground coriander
1 teaspoon sweet paprika
2 tablespoons olive oil
1 medium brown onion (150g), sliced thickly
1 cup (250ml) chicken stock
1 cinnamon stick
2 tablespoons honey
1/3 cup coarsely chopped fresh coriander
   (cilantro) leaves
1 tablespoon quince paste

1 Roll and tie lamb with kitchen string at 5cm
(2 inch) intervals. Using mortar and pestle, crush
garlic, coriander root and stem mixture, spices and
half the oil until almost smooth. Rub garlic mixture
all over lamb; cover, refrigerate 2 hours.
2 Heat remaining oil in large frying pan; cook lamb,
until browned all over. Remove from pan. Add onion
to same pan; cook, stirring, until onion softens.
3 Place stock, cinnamon and onion mixture in
4.5-litre (18-cup) slow cooker; top with lamb, drizzle
with honey. Season with salt and pepper. Cook,
covered, on low, 8 hours. Stand lamb 10 minutes;
stir quince paste into sauce.
4 Thickly slice lamb, serve with sauce; sprinkle
with chopped coriander.

prep + cook time 8 hours 25 minutes (+ refrigeration)
nutritional count per serving 31.5g total fat
(11.4g saturated fat); 2366kJ (566 cal);
15.8g carbohydrate; 54g protein; 1.9g fibre

• not suitable to freeze.

tip Cover and refrigerate lamb overnight at the end of step 1, if you like.
serving suggestion Serve lamb with couscous.

Curries

red curry lamb shanks

2 tablespoons vegetable oil
6 french-trimmed lamb shanks (2kg)
1 large kumara (orange sweet potato) (500g),
  chopped coarsely
3 fresh kaffir lime leaves, shredded thinly
1 large brown onion (200g), chopped finely
2 tablespoons red curry paste
1²/₃ cups (400ml) canned coconut cream
2 cups (500ml) chicken stock
2 tablespoons fish sauce
375g (12 ounces) snake beans, chopped coarsely
1 cup loosely packed fresh coriander
  (cilantro) leaves
2 tablespoons lime juice

1 Heat half the oil in large frying pan; cook lamb, in batches, until browned all over. Place lamb in 4.5-litre (18-cup) slow cooker, add kumara and lime leaves.
2 Heat remaining oil in same pan; cook onion, stirring, until soft. Add curry paste; cook, stirring, until fragrant. Add coconut cream; bring to the boil. Remove pan from heat; stir in stock and sauce, pour over lamb. Cook, covered, on low, 8 hours.
3 Add beans to cooker; cook, covered, on high, about 15 minutes. Stir in coriander and juice; season to taste.

prep + cook time 8 hours 40 minutes
nutritional count per serving 33.2g total fat (18g saturated fat); 2337kJ (559 cal); 17g carbohydrate; 45.6g protein; 6g fibre

tips If you can't find snake beans, use regular green beans instead.
Red curry paste is available in various strengths from supermarkets. Use whichever one suits your spice-level tolerance best.
serving suggestion Serve curry with steamed rice.

• suitable to freeze at the end of step 2.

lemon grass pork curry

serves 6

2 x 10cm (4 inch) sticks fresh lemon grass (40g),
  chopped coarsely
3 cloves garlic, quartered
4cm (1½ inch) piece fresh galangal (20g),
  sliced thinly
1 fresh small red thai (serrano) chilli,
  chopped coarsely
1 teaspoon ground turmeric
½ teaspoon ground cumin
¼ teaspoon ground cardamom
3 fresh kaffir lime leaves, shredded thinly
1 medium red onion (170g), chopped coarsely
½ cup (125ml) water
1 tablespoon peanut oil
1.2kg (2½ pounds) pork neck, chopped coarsely
3⅓ cups (800ml) canned coconut milk
3 baby eggplants (180g), sliced thickly
375g (12 ounces) baby carrots, halved lengthways
1 tablespoon fish sauce
2 tablespoons lime juice
½ cup loosely packed fresh coriander
  (cilantro) leaves

1 Blend or process lemon grass, garlic, galangal,
chilli, spices, lime leaves, onion and the water until
mixture is smooth.
2 Heat oil in medium frying pan; cook lemon grass
paste, stirring, about 5 minutes or until fragrant.
3 Transfer lemon grass mixture to 4.5-litre (18-cup)
slow cooker; stir in pork, coconut milk and eggplant.
Cook, covered, on low, 4 hours.
4 Add carrots; cook, covered, on low, 2 hours. Stir
in sauce and juice; season to taste. Sprinkle curry
with coriander.

prep + cook time 6 hours 30 minutes
nutritional count per serving 46.9g total fat
(30.2g saturated fat); 2759kJ (660 cal);
10.9g carbohydrate; 46.6g protein; 5.8g fibre

serving suggestion Serve curry with steamed rice.

• not suitable to freeze.

tamarind and coconut pork curry

serves 6

1 tablespoon peanut oil
1.2kg (2½ pounds) boned pork shoulder, chopped coarsely
1 medium brown onion (150g), chopped finely
2 cloves garlic, crushed
1 fresh long red chilli, sliced thinly
4cm (1½ inch) piece fresh ginger (20g), grated
2 teaspoons fenugreek seeds
1 teaspoon ground cumin
1 teaspoon ground ginger
½ teaspoon ground cinnamon
½ teaspoon ground cardamom
8 fresh curry leaves
1 tablespoon tamarind concentrate
1¼ cups (270ml) canned coconut cream
1 cup (250ml) chicken stock
185g (6 ounces) green beans, halved
1 cup (75g) toasted shredded coconut

1 Heat oil in large frying pan; cook pork, in batches, until browned. Remove from pan.
2 Cook onion, garlic, chilli and ginger in same heated pan, stirring, until onion softens. Add spices and curry leaves; cook, stirring, until fragrant.
3 Transfer onion mixture to 4.5-litre (18-cup) slow cooker; stir in pork, tamarind, coconut cream and stock. Cook, covered, on low, 6 hours.
4 Add beans and half the coconut; cook, covered, on high, 20 minutes or until beans are tender. Season to taste; sprinkle curry with remaining coconut.

prep + cook time 6 hours 40 minutes
nutritional count per serving 36.8g total fat (21.4g saturated fat); 2253kJ (539 cal); 5.2g carbohydrate; 45.6g protein; 4.1g fibre

serving suggestion Serve curry with steamed rice.

• not suitable to freeze.

chicken, lentil and pumpkin curry

serves 6

⅔ cup (130g) dried brown lentils
⅔ cup (130g) dried red lentils
1 tablespoon vegetable oil
1 large brown onion (200g), chopped finely
2 cloves garlic, crushed
2.5cm (1 inch) piece fresh ginger (10g), grated
2 teaspoons ground cumin
2 teaspoons ground coriander
2 teaspoons black mustard seeds
1 teaspoon ground turmeric
1 fresh long red chilli, chopped finely
3 cups (750ml) chicken stock
1kg (2 pounds) chicken thigh fillets,
  chopped coarsely
400g (14½ ounces) canned diced tomatoes
500g (1 pound) pumpkin, chopped coarsely
1¼ cups (270ml) canned coconut milk
155g (5 ounces) baby spinach leaves
½ cup coarsely chopped fresh coriander (cilantro)

1 Rinse lentils under cold water until water runs clear; drain. Heat oil in large frying pan; cook onion, garlic and ginger, stirring, until onion softens. Add spices and chilli; cook, stirring, until fragrant. Add stock; bring to the boil.
2 Pour stock mixture into 4.5-litre (18-cup) slow cooker; stir in chicken, undrained tomatoes, pumpkin and lentils. Cook, covered, on low, 7 hours.
3 Stir in coconut milk; cook, covered, on high, 15 minutes, stirring once. Stir in spinach and coriander. Season to taste.

prep + cook time 7 hours 40 minutes
nutritional count per serving 26.3g total fat (12.8g saturated fat); 2312kJ (553 cal); 27.6g carbohydrate; 47g protein; 10g fibre

serving suggestion Serve curry with chapatis and plain yogurt.

• suitable to freeze at the end of step 2.

creamy vegetable and almond korma

serves 6

½ cup (150g) korma paste
½ cup (60g) ground almonds
1 large brown onion (200g), sliced thinly
2 cloves garlic, crushed
½ cup (125ml) vegetable stock
½ cup (125ml) water
300ml (1⅓ cups) pouring cream
375g (12 ounces) baby carrots
125g (4 ounces) baby corn
500g (1 pound) baby potatoes, halved
375g (12 ounces) pumpkin, chopped coarsely
315g (10 ounces) cauliflower, cut into florets
6 medium yellow patty-pan squash (180g), halved
½ cup (60g) frozen peas
½ cup (70g) roasted slivered almonds
2 teaspoons black sesame seeds

1 Combine paste, ground almonds, onion, garlic, stock, the water, cream, carrots, corn, potato, pumpkin and cauliflower in 4.5-litre (18-cup) slow cooker. Cook, covered, on low, 6 hours.
2 Add squash and peas; cook, covered, on high, about 20 minutes. Season to taste. Sprinkle curry with nuts and seeds.

prep + cook time 6 hours 45 minutes
nutritional count per serving 42.8g total fat (16.2g saturated fat); 2429kJ (581 cal); 29.6g carbohydrate; 14.4g protein; 12.4g fibre

tip This is a mild curry. For more heat, serve curry sprinkled with some sliced fresh red chilli.
serving suggestion Serve korma with steamed rice, naan and yogurt.

• suitable to freeze at the end of step 1.

lamb rogan josh

serves 6

1.5kg (3¼ pounds) boned lamb shoulder,
  chopped coarsely
2 large brown onions (400g), sliced thinly
5cm (2 inch) piece fresh ginger (25g), grated
3 cloves garlic, crushed
½ cup (150g) rogan josh paste
2 tablespoons tomato paste
400g (14½ ounces) canned diced tomatoes
½ cup (125ml) beef stock
1 cinnamon stick
4 cardamom pods, bruised
2 dried bay leaves
½ cup loosely packed fresh coriander
  (cilantro) leaves

1 Combine lamb, onion, ginger, garlic, pastes,
undrained tomatoes, stock, cinnamon, cardamom
and bay leaves in 4.5-litre (18-cup) slow cooker.
Cook, covered, on low, 8 hours. Season to taste.
2 Sprinkle curry with coriander.

prep + cook time 8 hours 20 minutes
nutritional count per serving 30.1g total fat
(10.8g saturated fat); 2249kJ (538 cal);
8.8g carbohydrate; 55.7g protein; 5.1g fibre

serving suggestion Serve lamb with steamed rice,
naan and yogurt.

• suitable to freeze at the end of step 1.

indian vegetable curry

serves 6

1 tablespoon vegetable oil
1 medium leek (350g), sliced thickly
2 cloves garlic, crushed
2 teaspoons black mustard seeds
2 teaspoons ground cumin
2 teaspoons garam masala
1 teaspoon ground turmeric
1½ cups (375ml) vegetable stock
400g (14½ ounces) canned diced tomatoes
1 large kumara (orange sweet potato) (500g),
   chopped coarsely
1 large carrot (180g), chopped coarsely
1⅔ cups (400ml) canned coconut milk
375g (12 ounces) brussels sprouts, halved
400g (15 ounces) canned chickpeas
   (garbanzo beans), rinsed, drained
155g (5 ounces) baby spinach leaves
½ cup coarsely chopped fresh coriander (cilantro)

1 Heat oil in large frying pan; cook leek and garlic, stirring, until leek softens. Add spices; cook, stirring, until fragrant. Add stock; bring to the boil.
2 Pour stock mixture into 4.5-litre (18-cup) slow cooker; stir in undrained tomatoes, kumara, carrot and coconut milk. Cook, covered, on low, 4 hours.
3 Add sprouts and chickpeas to curry. Cook, covered, on high, about 40 minutes or until sprouts are just tender.
4 Stir in spinach and coriander. Season to taste.

prep + cook time 5 hours
nutritional count per serving 18.7g total fat
(12.8g saturated fat); 1388kJ (332 cal);
25.4g carbohydrate; 10.7g protein; 10.6g fibre

• suitable to freeze at the end of step 3.

serving suggestion Serve curry with naan bread and lemon wedges.

butter chicken

serves 6

12 chicken thigh cutlets (2.4kg), skin removed
2 tablespoons lemon juice
1 teaspoon chilli powder
¾ cup (200g) greek-style yogurt
5cm (2 inch) piece fresh ginger (25g), grated
2 teaspoons garam masala
45g (1½ ounces) butter
1 tablespoon vegetable oil
1 medium brown onion (150g), chopped finely
4 cloves garlic, crushed
1 teaspoon ground coriander
1 teaspoon ground cumin
1 teaspoon sweet paprika
2 tablespoons tomato paste
1⅔ cups (410g) canned tomato puree
⅔ cup (160ml) chicken stock
2 tablespoons honey
1 cinnamon stick
⅓ cup (80ml) pouring cream
⅓ cup (80g) ricotta cheese
½ cup loosely packed fresh coriander
  (cilantro) leaves

1   Combine chicken, juice and chilli powder in large bowl. Cover, refrigerate 30 minutes.
2   Stir yogurt, ginger and half the garam masala into chicken mixture.
3   Heat butter and oil in large frying pan; cook chicken, in batches, until browned all over. Transfer chicken to 4.5-litre (18-cup) slow cooker. Add onion and garlic to same pan; cook, stirring, until onion softens. Add remaining garam masala and ground spices; cook, stirring, until fragrant. Remove from heat; stir in tomato paste, puree, stock, honey and cinnamon. Transfer tomato mixture to slow cooker. Cook, covered, on low, 4 hours.
4   Stir in cream; season to taste.
5   Serve topped with ricotta and coriander leaves.

prep + cook time 4 hours 30 minutes (+ refrigeration)
nutritional count per serving 39.3g total fat
(17g saturated fat); 2750kJ (658 cal);
17.9g carbohydrate; 57.8g protein; 2.6g fibre

serving suggestion Serve chicken with steamed basmati rice and warm naan bread.

• suitable to freeze at the end of step 3.

old-fashioned curried sausages

serves 6

12 thick beef sausages (1.8kg)
1 tablespoon vegetable oil
2 medium brown onions (300g), sliced thinly
2 tablespoons mild curry powder
400g (14½ ounces) canned diced tomatoes
1 cup (250ml) beef stock
1 cup (250ml) water
4 medium potatoes (800g), unpeeled, cut into thick wedges
1 cup (120g) frozen peas, thawed
½ cup (80g) sultanas

1 Place sausages in large saucepan, add enough cold water to cover sausages; bring to the boil. Boil, uncovered, 2 minutes; drain.
2 Heat oil in same pan; cook onion, stirring, until softened. Add curry powder; cook, stirring, until fragrant. Remove from heat; stir in undrained tomatoes, stock and the water.
3 Place potatoes in 4.5-litre (18-cup) slow cooker; top with sausages and onion mixture. Cook, covered, on low, 8 hours.
4 Stir in peas and sultanas. Season to taste.

prep + cook time 8 hours 20 minutes
nutritional count per serving 79.8g total fat (37g saturated fat); 4435kJ (1061 cal); 40g carbohydrate; 41.3g protein; 13.7g fibre

serving suggestion Serve with crusty bread.

• not suitable to freeze.

spinach dhal

serves 6

500g (1 pound) yellow split peas
45g (1½ ounces) ghee
2 medium brown onions (300g), chopped finely
3 cloves garlic, crushed
4cm (1½ inch) piece fresh ginger (20g), grated
1 fresh long green chilli, chopped finely
2 tablespoons black mustard seeds
1 teaspoon cumin seeds
1 tablespoon ground coriander
2 teaspoons ground turmeric
1 teaspoon garam masala
800g (28 ounces) canned diced tomatoes
3 cups (750ml) vegetable stock
1½ cups (375ml) water
1 teaspoon caster (superfine) sugar
4 medium silver beet (swiss chard) leaves (320g),
   stems removed, chopped coarsely

1 Rinse split peas under cold water until water runs clear; drain.
2 Heat ghee in large frying pan; cook onion, garlic, ginger and chilli, stirring, until onion softens. Add seeds and spices; cook, stirring, until fragrant. Place onion mixture into 4.5-litre (18-cup) slow cooker; stir in undrained tomatoes, stock, the water, sugar and peas. Cook, covered, on low, 10 hours.
3 Stir in silver beet; season to taste.

prep + cook time 10 hours 20 minutes
nutritional count per serving 10.1g total fat (5.4g saturated fat); 1689kJ (404 cal); 48.2g carbohydrate; 23.3g protein; 12.5g fibre

serving suggestion Serve dhal topped with fried or caramelised onions.
• suitable to freeze at the end of step 2.

spiced chicken in coconut sauce

serves 6

1 tablespoon peanut oil
3 chicken thigh fillets (660g), halved
6 chicken drumsticks (900g)
2 medium brown onions (300g), chopped coarsely
1 cup (250ml) chicken stock
1⅔ cups (400ml) canned coconut milk
3 fresh kaffir lime leaves, shredded thinly
315g (10 ounces) green beans, chopped coarsely
12 fresh thai eggplants (350g), halved
¾ cup loosely packed fresh coriander
   (cilantro) leaves
SPICE PASTE
4 shallots (100g), quartered
2 cloves garlic, chopped coarsely
5cm (2 inch) piece fresh ginger (25g),
   chopped coarsely
2 teaspoons ground cumin
2 teaspoons ground coriander
2 teaspoons ground turmeric
3 fresh small red thai (serrano) chillies,
   chopped coarsely
2 tablespoons fish sauce
2 tablespoons peanut oil
2 tablespoons lime juice
1 tablespoon grated palm sugar

1 Make spice paste.
2 Heat half the oil in large frying pan; cook chicken, in batches, until browned all over, place in 4.5-litre (18-cup) slow cooker. Heat remaining oil in same pan; cook onion, stirring, until soft. Add spice paste; cook, stirring, until fragrant. Add stock; bring to the boil.
3 Remove from heat; stir in coconut milk and lime leaves, pour over chicken. Cook, covered, on low, 7 hours.
4 Add beans and eggplant, cook, covered, on high, about 20 minutes or until vegetables are tender. Season to taste; sprinkle with coriander.
spice paste Blend or process ingredients until mixture is smooth.

prep + cook time 7 hours 45 minutes
nutritional count per serving 41.9g total fat (19.4g saturated fat); 2508kJ (600 cal); 11.6g carbohydrate; 42.5g protein; 5.5g fibre

• suitable to freeze at the end of step 3.

serving suggestion Serve chicken with steamed rice and lime wedges.

duck vindaloo

serves 6

1.8kg (3¾ pound) whole duck
¼ cup (35g) plain (all-purpose) flour
1 tablespoon peanut oil
2 teaspoons cumin seeds
2 teaspoons fenugreek seeds
1 teaspoon ground coriander
1 teaspoon ground turmeric
½ teaspoon ground cardamom
4 fresh small red thai (serrano) chillies,
  chopped coarsely
3 cloves garlic, quartered
2.5cm (1 inch) piece fresh ginger (15g),
  sliced thinly
⅓ cup (80ml) white vinegar
½ cup (125ml) chicken stock
1 medium red onion (170g), chopped finely
4 medium potatoes (800g), chopped coarsely
2 tablespoons chicken gravy powder
2 tablespoons water
½ cup loosely packed fresh coriander
  (cilantro) leaves

1 Rinse duck under cold water; pat dry. Cut duck into six serving-sized pieces. Toss duck in flour, shake off excess. Heat oil in large frying pan; cook duck, in batches, until browned. Transfer to 4.5-litre (18-cup) slow cooker.

2 Meanwhile, dry-fry spices in small frying pan until fragrant; cool. Blend or process spices, chilli, garlic, ginger and vinegar until smooth.

3 Stir spice mixture into cooker with stock, onion and potato. Cook, covered, on low, 6 hours. Season to taste.

4 Transfer duck and potato to serving plate. Skim excess fat from sauce. Stir combined gravy powder and the water into sauce in slow cooker. Cook, covered, on high, about 10 minutes or until the sauce thickens.

5 Drizzle sauce over duck; sprinkle with coriander.

prep + cook time 6 hours 45 minutes
nutritional count per serving 66.5g total fat (19.6g saturated fat); 3323kJ (795 cal); 22.7g carbohydrate; 26.7g protein; 3g fibre

• not suitable to freeze.

tip This is a mild vindaloo. If you like it hotter, add more fresh chillies when you make the paste.
serving suggestion Serve vindaloo with steamed rice.

Accompaniments

soft polenta Combine 3 cups water and 2 cups vegetable stock in large saucepan; bring to the boil. Gradually stir in 2 cups polenta. Simmer, stirring, about 10 minutes or until polenta thickens. Add 1 cup milk, 30g (1 ounce) butter and ¼ cup finely grated parmesan cheese; stir until cheese melts.

parsnip mash Boil, steam or microwave 1kg (2 pounds) chopped parsnip until tender; drain. Mash parsnip in medium bowl with ¾ cup hot milk until smooth; stir in 2 crushed garlic cloves and 40g (1¼ ounces) soft butter.
(Note: the same amount of kumara, celeriac or pumpkin can be used instead of parsnip.)

roast potatoes Preheat oven to 180°C/350°F. Lightly oil oven tray. Boil, steam or microwave 6 halved medium potatoes for 5 minutes; drain. Pat dry with absorbent paper; cool 10 minutes. Gently rake rounded sides of potatoes with tines of fork; place potato, in single layer, cut-side down, on oven tray. Brush with 2 tablespoons olive oil; roast, uncovered, in oven, 50 minutes or until browned lightly and crisp.

couscous Combine 1½ cups couscous with 1½ cups boiling water in large heatproof bowl, cover; stand about 5 minutes or until water is absorbed, fluffing with fork occasionally. Stir in 60g (2 ounces) finely shredded baby spinach leaves or some coarsely chopped fresh herbs of your choice, or 2 finely chopped green onions (scallions).

creamy mashed potatoes Boil, steam or microwave 750g (1½ pounds) coarsely chopped potatoes until tender; drain. Mash potato with 60g (2 ounces) soft butter and ½ cup hot pouring cream in medium bowl until smooth.

steamed gai lan in oyster sauce Boil, steam or microwave 1kg (2 pounds) halved gai lan until tender; drain. Heat 1 tablespoon peanut oil in wok; stir-fry gai lan, 2 tablespoons oyster sauce and 1 tablespoon light soy sauce about 2 minutes or until mixture is heated through.

pilaf Melt 30g (1 ounce) butter in medium saucepan; cook 1 crushed garlic clove, stirring, until fragrant. Add 1 cup basmati rice; cook, stirring, 1 minute. Add 1 cup chicken stock and 1 cup water; bring to the boil. Simmer, covered, about 20 minutes or until rice is tender. Remove from heat; fluff rice with fork. Stir in ¼ cup coarsely chopped fresh flat-leaf parsley and ¼ cup roasted flaked almonds.

tomato and herb salad Place 5 coarsely chopped medium tomatoes, 2 tablespoons chopped fresh mint, ¼ cup chopped fresh flat-leaf parsley and 2 tablespoons chopped fresh dill in medium bowl. Place 2 cloves crushed garlic, 2 tablespoons lemon juice, 1 tablespoon olive oil and 2 teaspoons white vinegar in screw-top jar; shake well. Drizzle dressing over salad; toss to combine.

Desserts

vanilla and red wine poached pears serves 6

6 medium firm pears (1.4kg)
2 cups (500ml) dry red wine
1½ cups (375ml) water
5cm (2 inch) piece orange rind
½ cup (125ml) orange juice
1 cup (220g) caster (superfine) sugar
1 vanilla bean
1 cinnamon stick

1 Peel pears, leaving stems intact.
2 Combine wine, the water, rind, juice and sugar in 4.5-litre (18-cup) slow cooker. Halve vanilla bean lengthways, scrape seeds into slow cooker; add vanilla bean and cinnamon stick.
3 Lay pears down in cooker to cover in wine mixture. Cook, covered, on high, about 4½ hours or until pears are tender. Place 1 cup of the poaching liquid in small saucepan; bring to the boil. Boil, uncovered, about 7 minutes or until syrup is reduced by about half; cool.
4 Meanwhile, place pears in large deep bowl; add remaining poaching liquid, cool.
5 Serve pears drizzled with syrup.

prep + cook time 4 hours 50 minutes (+ cooling)
nutritional count per serving 0.2g total fat
(0g saturated fat); 1225kJ (293 cal);
55.9g carbohydrate; 0.8g protein; 3.3g fibre

tips Store leftover poaching liquid in refrigerator for up to 1 month. Use for poaching more pears or stone fruit. We used packham pears in this recipe.
serving suggestion Serve with whipped cream or vanilla ice-cream.

• not suitable to freeze.

nutty baked apples with butterscotch sauce serves 6

6 small green apples (780g)
90g (3 ounces) butter, chopped finely
¼ cup (35g) slivered almonds
¼ cup (30g) finely chopped walnuts
½ teaspoon ground cinnamon
1 cup (220g) firmly packed light brown sugar
¾ cup (180ml) pouring cream
½ cup (125ml) apple juice

1 Core unpeeled apples about three-quarters of the way through, making hole 4cm (1½ inches) in diameter. Use small sharp knife to score around centre of each apple.
2 Combine one-third of the butter with nuts, cinnamon and ¼ cup of the sugar in small bowl. Press mixture into apple cavities.

3 Combine cream, juice, remaining butter and sugar in 4.5-litre (18-cup) slow cooker. Stand apples upright in sauce. Cook, covered, on high, about 2½ hours, turning apples once, or until apples are tender.
4 Remove apples from cooker; cover to keep warm. Drain sauce into small saucepan; bring to the boil. Boil, uncovered, about 5 minutes or until sauce is thickened slightly.
5 Serve apples drizzled with sauce.

prep + cook time 3 hours 20 minutes
nutritional count per serving 32.1g total fat (17.1g saturated fat); 2107kJ (504 cal); 50.1g carbohydrate; 2.9g protein; 2.8g fibre

tip Make sure the apples don't touch the side of the slow cooker.
serving suggestion Serve apples with custard, cream or ice-cream.

• not suitable to freeze.

fig and cranberry bread pudding

serves 6

315g (10 ounces) crusty white bread, sliced thickly
½ cup (160g) fig jam (conserve)
½ cup (65g) finely chopped dried cranberries
2½ cups (625ml) milk
2⅓ cups (600ml) pouring cream
½ cup (110g) caster (superfine) sugar
1 teaspoon vanilla extract
6 eggs

1   Grease 4.5-litre (18-cup) slow cooker bowl. Spread bread slices with jam. Layer bread, overlapping, in cooker bowl; sprinkle with cranberries.
2   Combine milk, cream, sugar and extract in medium saucepan; bring to the boil. Whisk eggs in medium bowl; gradually whisk in hot milk mixture. Pour custard over bread; stand 5 minutes.
3   Cook, covered, on low, about 4 hours (do not lift the lid during the cooking process, *see tip*).
4   Remove bowl from cooker. Stand pudding 5 minutes before serving. Serve pudding dusted with a little sifted icing sugar.

prep + cook time 4 hours 20 minutes
nutritional count per serving 54.6g total fat (33.2g saturated fat); 3670kJ (878 cal); 78.8g carbohydrate; 17.2g protein; 2.9g fibre

tips It's important not to lift the lid during the cooking of the pudding, as the condensation runs down the side of the cooker and causes damp patches on the pudding.
We used a small vienna loaf in this recipe.
serving suggestion Serve pudding with cream and/or ice-cream.

• not suitable to freeze.

steamed Christmas pudding

serves 12

2½ cups (375g) chopped mixed dried fruit
¾ cup (120g) finely chopped dried seedless dates
½ cup (65g) finely chopped dried cranberries
¾ cup (180ml) water
1 cup (220g) firmly packed dark brown sugar
90g (3 ounces) butter, chopped coarsely
1 teaspoon bicarbonate of soda (baking soda)
2 eggs, beaten lightly
¾ cup (110g) plain (all-purpose) flour
¾ cup (110g) self-raising flour
1 teaspoon mixed spice
½ teaspoon ground cinnamon
¼ cup (60ml) dark rum

1 Combine fruit, the water, sugar and butter in medium saucepan. Stir over heat until butter melts and sugar dissolves; bring to the boil. Reduce heat; simmer, uncovered, 5 minutes. Transfer mixture to large heatproof bowl, stir in soda; cool 10 minutes.
2 Stir eggs, sifted dry ingredients and rum into the fruit mixture.
3 Grease 2-litre (8-cup) pudding steamer; spoon mixture into steamer. Top with pleated baking paper and foil; secure with kitchen string or lid.
4 Place pudding in 4.5-litre (18-cup) slow cooker with enough boiling water to come halfway up side of steamer. Cook, covered, on high, 5 hours, replenishing with boiling water as necessary to maintain level.
5 Remove pudding from cooker, stand 10 minutes before turning onto plate.

prep + cook time 5 hours 30 minutes
nutritional count per serving 7.6g total fat
(4.5g saturated fat); 1463kJ (350 cal);
61.5g carbohydrate; 4.1g protein; 3.7g fibre

• suitable to freeze at the end of step 5; pudding can be frozen as a whole pudding, or in serving-sized wedges.

tip The pleated paper and foil allow for the pudding mixture to rise.
serving suggestion Serve with cream or custard.

creamy rice pudding with cinnamon sugar serves 6

1 cup (200g) uncooked white medium-grain rice
1.25 litres (5 cups) milk
½ cup (110g) caster (superfine) sugar
5cm (2 inch) piece orange rind
1 vanilla bean
2 tablespoons caster (superfine) sugar, extra
1 teaspoon ground cinnamon

1 Combine rice, milk, sugar and rind in 4.5-litre (18-cup) slow cooker. Halve vanilla bean lengthways; scrape seeds into cooker, add vanilla bean.
2 Cook, covered, on low, 6 hours, stirring twice, or until rice is tender. Discard vanilla bean and rind.
3 Combine extra sugar and cinnamon in small bowl, sprinkle over pudding.

prep + cook time 6 hours 10 minutes
nutritional count per serving 8.3g total fat (5.4g saturated fat); 1513kJ (362 cal); 61.5g carbohydrate; 9.3g protein; 0.3g fibre

tip The vanilla bean can be reused; wash and dry well, store in an airtight container or add to a container of sugar for vanilla-scented sugar.
serving suggestion Serve warm pudding with canned, fresh or stewed fruit drizzled with cream. (We stewed 150g frozen raspberries with ¼ cup caster sugar and 1 tablespoon of water.)

• not suitable to freeze.

chocolate self-saucing pudding

serves 6

90g (3 ounces) butter
¾ cup (180ml) milk
1 teaspoon vanilla extract
1 cup (220g) caster (superfine) sugar
1½ cups (225g) self-raising flour
2 tablespoons cocoa powder
1 egg, beaten lightly
1 cup (220g) firmly packed light brown sugar
2 tablespoons cocoa powder, extra
2½ cups (625ml) boiling water

1 Grease 4.5-litre (18-cup) slow cooker bowl.
2 Melt butter in milk over low heat in medium saucepan. Remove from heat; cool 5 minutes. Stir in extract and caster sugar, then sifted flour and cocoa, and egg. Spread mixture into cooker bowl.
3 Sift brown sugar and extra cocoa evenly over mixture; gently pour boiling water evenly over mixture. Cook, covered, on high, about 2½ hours or until centre is firm.
4 Remove bowl from cooker. Stand pudding 5 minutes before serving.

prep + cook time 2 hours 50 minutes
nutritional count per serving 15.5g total fat (9.6g saturated fat); 2424kJ (580 cal); 101.3g carbohydrate; 6.9g protein; 1.6g fibre

serving suggestion Serve pudding, hot or warm, dusted with a little sifted icing sugar, and with cream and/or ice-cream.

• not suitable to freeze.

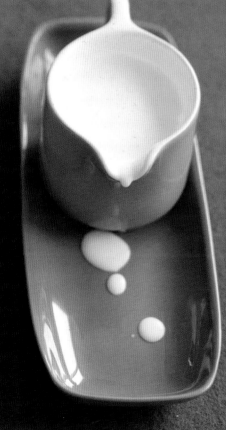

mandarin and almond pudding

4 small mandarins (mandarin oranges) (400g)
4 eggs
²/₃ cup (150g) caster (superfine) sugar
1¹/₃ cups (160g) ground almonds
²/₃ cup (100g) self-raising flour

1 Place washed unpeeled mandarins in 4.5-litre (18-cup) slow cooker; cover with hot water. Cook, covered, on high, 2 hours.
2 Trim ends from mandarins; discard. Halve mandarins; remove and discard seeds. Process mandarins, including rind, until mixture is pulpy.
3 Grease 2-litre (8-cup) pudding steamer.
4 Beat eggs and sugar in small bowl with electric mixer until thick and creamy; fold in ground almonds, sifted flour and mandarin pulp. Spoon mixture into steamer. Top with pleated baking paper and foil; secure with kitchen string or lid.
5 Place pudding in cooker with enough boiling water to come halfway up side of steamer. Cook, covered, on high, 3 hours, replenishing with boiling water as necessary to maintain level. Stand pudding 5 minutes before turning onto plate.

prep + cook time 5 hours 30 minutes
nutritional count per serving 13.9g total fat (1.6g saturated fat); 1246kJ (298 cal); 32.5g carbohydrate; 9g protein; 3.2g fibre

• not suitable to freeze.

tip The pleated paper and foil simply allow space for the pudding mixture to rise.
serving suggestion Serve with cream, custard or ice-cream.

Glossary

ALLSPICE also known as pimento or jamaican pepper; available whole or ground. Tastes like a blend of cinnamon, clove and nutmeg – all spices.

ALMONDS, GROUND also known as almond meal; nuts are powdered to a coarse flour-like texture.

BACON SLICES also known as bacon rashers; made from cured, smoked pork.

BEANS
black turtle also known as black or black kidney beans; an earthy-flavoured dried bean completely different from the better-known chinese black beans (which are fermented soya beans).
cannellini small white bean that is similar in appearance and flavour to haricot, great northern and navy beans, all of which can be substituted for the other.
green also known as french or string beans, this long thin fresh bean is consumed in its entirety once cooked.
kidney medium-sized red bean, slightly floury in texture yet sweet in flavour.
snake long (about 40cm), thin, round, fresh green beans; Asian in origin, with a taste similar to green or french beans. They are also known as yard-long beans because of their (pre-metric) length.

BEEF
brisket a cheaper cut from the belly; can be bought with or without bones as a joint for slow-roasting, or for stewing and casseroling as cubes or mince.
blade taken from the shoulder; isn't as tender as other cuts of beef, it needs slow-roasting to achieve best results.
cheeks the cheek muscle of a cow. It's a very tough and lean cut of meat and is most often used for braising or slow cooking to produce a tender result.
chuck from the neck and shoulder of the beef; tends to be chewy but flavourful and inexpensive. A good cut for stewing or braising.
corned silverside also known as topside roast; sold vacuum-sealed in brine.
gravy beef also known as beef shin or shank, cut from the lower shin of a cow.
osso buco literally meaning 'bone with a hole', osso buco is cut from the shin of the hind leg. It is also known as knuckle.
sausages seasoned and spiced minced beef mixed with cereal and packed into casings. Also known as snags or bangers.
shank, see gravy beef (above).
short ribs cut from the rib section; are usually larger, more tender and meatier than pork spare ribs.

BEETROOT also known as red beets or beets; firm, round root vegetable.

BICARBONATE OF SODA also known as baking or carb soda; a leavening agent.

BREADCRUMBS, STALE one- or two-day-old bread made into crumbs by grating, blending or processing.

BUK CHOY also known as bok choy, pak choi, chinese white cabbage or chinese chard; has a fresh, mild mustard taste.

BUTTER use salted or unsalted (sweet) butter; 125g equals one stick (4 ounces).

CAPERS, BABY those picked early, are very small, fuller-flavoured and more expensive than the full-size one. Capers must be rinsed well before using.

CARAWAY a member of the parsley family; is available in seed or ground form. Has a pungent aroma and a distinctly sweet, but tangy, flavour.

CARDAMOM can be purchased in pod, seed or ground form. Has a distinctive aromatic, sweetly rich flavour.

CARROTS, BABY small, sweet, and sold in bunches with the tops still attached.

CAVOLO NERO, or tuscan cabbage, is a staple in Tuscan country cooking. It has long, narrow, wrinkled leaves and a rich and astringent, mild cabbage flavour. It doesn't lose its volume like silver beet or spinach when cooked, but it does need longer cooking.

CHICKEN
drumsticks leg with skin and bone intact.
thigh cutlets thigh with skin and centre bone intact; sometimes found skinned with bone intact.
thigh fillets thigh with skin and centre bone removed.

CHILLI available in many types and sizes. Use rubber gloves when seeding and chopping fresh chillies as they can burn your skin. Removing membranes and seeds lessens the heat level.
cayenne pepper dried, long, thin-fleshed, extremely hot ground red chilli.
flakes dried, deep-red, dehydrated chilli slices and whole seeds.
long green any unripened chilli.
long red available both fresh and dried; a generic term used for any moderately hot, long (6cm-8cm), thin chilli.
powder can be used as a substitute for fresh chillies (½ teaspoon ground chilli powder to 1 medium chopped fresh chilli).

CHINESE COOKING WINE also known as hao hsing or chinese rice wine; made from fermented rice, wheat, sugar and salt with a 13.5 per cent alcohol content. Found in Asian food shops; if you can't find it, replace with mirin or sherry.

COCOA POWDER also known as cocoa; dried, unsweetened, roasted then ground cocoa beans (cacao seeds).

CORIANDER the leaves, stems and roots of coriander are used in Thai cooking; wash roots well before using. Is also available ground or as seeds; do not substitute these for fresh coriander as the tastes are completely different.

CRANBERRIES, DRIED have the same slightly sour, succulent flavour as fresh cranberries. Available in supermarkets.

CREAM we use fresh cream, also known as pure cream and pouring cream, unless otherwise stated.

CUMIN also known as zeera or comino; has a spicy, nutty flavour, and is available in seed form or dried and ground.

CURRY LEAVES available fresh or dried and have a mild curry flavour; use like bay leaves.

CURRY PASTES some recipes in this book call for commercially prepared pastes of varying strengths and flavours. Use whichever one you feel best suits your spice-level tolerance.
korma paste a mix of mostly heat-free spices, forms the base of a mild, almost nutty, slow-cooked curry.
powder a blend of ground spices that include chilli, cinnamon, coriander, mace, fennel, fenugreek, cumin, cardamom and turmeric. Can be mild or hot.
red probably the most popular curry paste; a hot blend of red chilli, garlic, shallot, lemon grass, salt, galangal, shrimp paste, kaffir lime peel, coriander, cumin and paprika. It is milder than the hotter Thai green curry paste.
rogan josh paste a medium-hot blend that is a specialty of Kashmir in northern India. It features tomatoes, fenugreek, coriander, paprika and cumin.

EGGPLANT also known as aubergine.
baby also known as finger or japanese eggplant; very small and slender so can be used without disgorging.

FENUGREEK a member of the pea family, the seeds have a bitter taste; the ground seeds are a traditional ingredient in Indian curries, powders and pastes.

FIVE-SPICE POWDER (chinese five-spice) a fragrant mixture of ground cinnamon, cloves, star anise, sichuan pepper and fennel seeds.

FLOUR
cornflour also known as cornstarch; used as a thickening agent. Available as 100% maize (corn) and wheaten cornflour.
plain all-purpose flour made from wheat.
self-raising plain flour sifted with baking powder in the proportion of 1 cup flour to 2 teaspoons baking powder.

GARAM MASALA a blend of spices including cardamom, cinnamon, cloves, coriander, fennel and cumin, roasted and ground together. Black pepper and chilli can be added for a hotter version.

GHEE a type of clarified butter where the milk solids are cooked until they are a golden brown, which imparts a nutty flavour and sweet aroma; this fat can be heated to a high temperature without burning. Available from the refrigerated section of supermarkets.

GINGER also known as green or root ginger; the thick root of a tropical plant.
ground also known as powdered ginger; used as a flavouring in cakes and pies but cannot be substituted for fresh ginger.

GRAVY POWDER an instant gravy mix made with browned flour. Plain flour can be used instead for thickening. Available from supermarkets in a variety of flavours.

HARISSA a Moroccan sauce or paste made from dried chillies, cumin, garlic, oil and caraway seeds; used as a rub for meats, a sauce and dressing ingredient, or as a condiment eaten on its own. It is available from Middle-Eastern food shops and supermarkets.

HONEYCOMB TRIPE check with the butcher to make sure the tripe has been cleaned and blanched. We suggest you blanch the tripe again before cutting it into pieces. You might have to order the tripe from the butcher in advance.

HORSERADISH CREAM a paste of grated horseradish, mustard seeds, oil and sugar.

KUMARA Polynesian name of an orange-fleshed sweet potato; it is not a yam.

LAMB
forequarter chops from the shoulder end of the sheep.
shanks, french-trimmed also known as drumsticks or frenched shanks; the gristle and narrow end of the bone is discarded then the remaining meat trimmed.

shoulder boned from the shoulder. Is very hard to carve with the bone in; to make carving easier, butchers will bone it and sell it as a boneless rolled shoulder.

LEEK a member of the onion family; looks like a giant green onion but is more subtle and mild in flavour.
baby, or pencil leeks, essentially young, slender leeks available early in the season, can be cooked and eaten like asparagus.

LENTILS (red, brown, yellow) dried pulses identified by and named after their colour.

MARSALA a sweet, fortified wine to which additional alcohol has been added, most commonly in the form of brandy. It is available in a range of styles, from sweet to dry.

MINCE also known as ground meat.

MIXED DRIED FRUIT a mix of sultanas, raisins, currants, mixed peel and cherries.

MIXED SPICE a blend of ground spices usually consisting of cinnamon, allspice and nutmeg.

MOROCCAN SEASONING available from most Middle-Eastern food stores, spice shops and major supermarkets. Turmeric, cinnamon and cumin add authentic Moroccan flavouring to dishes.

MUSHROOMS
button small, cultivated white mushrooms with a mild flavour.
portobello mature swiss browns. Large, dark brown mushrooms with full-bodied flavour; ideal for filling or barbecuing.

MUSSELS must be tightly closed when bought, indicating they are alive. Before cooking, scrub the shells with a strong brush and remove the "beards". Discard shells that do not open during cooking.

MUSTARD
dijon pale brown, distinctively flavoured, fairly mild-tasting french mustard.
seeds, black also known as brown mustard seeds; more pungent than the yellow (or white) seeds used in prepared mustards.
wholegrain also known as seeded. A french-style coarse-grain mustard made from crushed mustard seeds and dijon-style french mustard.

OILS
olive made from ripened olives. Extra virgin and virgin are the best, while extra light or light refers to taste, not fat levels.
peanut pressed from ground peanuts; most commonly used oil in Asian cooking because of its high smoke point (capacity to handle high heat without burning).

sesame made from roasted, crushed, white sesame seeds; a flavouring rather than a cooking medium.
vegetable oils sourced from plants rather than animal fats.

OLIVES
black have a richer and more mellow flavour than the green ones and are softer in texture. Sold either plain or in a piquant marinade.
green those harvested before fully ripened and are, as a rule, denser and more bitter than their black relatives.

ONIONS
baby also known as pickling onions and cocktail onions; are baby brown onions, though are larger than shallots.
brown and white are interchangeable, however, white onions have a more pungent flesh.
red also known as spanish, red spanish or bermuda onion; a sweet-flavoured, large, purple-red onion.

PAPRIKA ground, dried, sweet red capsicum (bell pepper); there are many types available, including sweet, hot, mild and smoked.

PATTY-PAN SQUASH also known as crookneck or custard marrow pumpkins; a round, slightly flat summer squash being yellow to pale-green in colour and having a scalloped edge. It has a firm white flesh and a distinct flavour.

PEPPERCORNS, BLACK picked when the berry is not quite ripe, then dried until it shrivels and the skin turns dark brown/black. It's the strongest flavoured of the three (white, green and black) – slightly hot with a hint of sweetness.

PISTACHIOS delicately flavoured green nuts inside hard off-white shells. Available salted or unsalted. We always use shelled nuts in our recipes.

POLENTA also known as cornmeal; a flour-like cereal made of dried corn (maize) sold ground in several different textures; also the name of the dish made from it.

PORK
hand of pickled pork the "hand" is a portion of leg and breast. You may need to order this from the butcher in advance.
ham hock the lower portion of the leg; includes the meat, fat and bone. Most have been cured, smoked or both, but fresh hocks are sometimes available.
neck sometimes called pork scotch; a boneless cut from the foreloin.

shoulder joint sold with bone in or out.
spare ribs American-style spareribs; well-trimmed mid-loin ribs.

POTATOES, BABY NEW also known as chats; not a separate variety but an early harvest with very thin skin; good unpeeled steamed and eaten, hot or cold, in salads.

PRAWNS also known as shrimp.

PRESERVED LEMON RIND a North African specialty; lemons are quartered and preserved in salt and lemon juice or water. To use, remove and discard pulp, squeeze juice from rind, rinse rind well; slice thinly. Sold in delicatessens and major supermarkets.

RAISINS dried sweet grapes.

RAS EL HANOUT a classic spice blend used in Moroccan cooking. The name means 'top of the shop' and is the very best spice blend a spice merchant has to offer. Most versions contain over a dozen spices, including cardamom, mace, nutmeg, cinnamon and ground chilli.

RICE
basmati a white, fragrant long-grained rice. Wash several times before cooking.
medium-grain previously sold as calrose rice; extremely versatile rice that can be substituted for short- or long-grain rices if necessary.

RISONI small, rice-shaped pasta similar to orzo; used in soups and salads.

ROMANO CHEESE a hard, sheep's- or cow's-milk cheese. Straw-coloured and grainy in texture, it's mainly used for grating. Parmesan can be substituted.

SAFFRON available in strands (threads) or ground form; imparts a yellow-orange colour to food once infused. Quality varies greatly; the best is the most expensive spice in the world. Should be stored in the freezer.

SAUCES
char siu a Chinese barbecue sauce made from sugar, water, salt, fermented soya bean paste, honey, soy sauce, malt syrup and spices. Found at most supermarkets.
fish also called nam pla or nuoc nam; made from pulverised salted fermented fish, most often anchovies. Has a very pungent smell and strong taste, so use according to your taste level.
oyster Asian in origin, this rich, brown sauce is made from oysters and their brine, cooked with salt and soy sauce, and thickened with starches.

soy also known as sieu, is made from fermented soya beans. Several variations are available in most supermarkets and Asian food stores. We use a mild Japanese variety in our recipes; possibly the best table soy and the one to choose if you only want one variety.
light soy a fairly thin, pale but salty tasting sauce; used in dishes in which the natural colour of the ingredients is to be maintained. Not to be confused with salt-reduced or low-sodium soy sauces.
tamari a thick, dark soy sauce made mainly from soya beans without the wheat used in standard soy sauces.
tomato pasta made from a blend of tomatoes, herbs and spices.
worcestershire a dark-coloured condiment made from garlic, soy sauce, tamarind, onions, molasses, lime, anchovies, vinegar and seasonings.

SAUSAGES minced meat seasoned with salt and spices, mixed with cereal and packed into casings. Also known as snags or bangers.
italian pork a pork sausage often added to pasta sauces. Varieties include sweet Italian sausage, which is flavoured with garlic and fennel seed, and hot Italian sausage, which has chilli.

SOUR CREAM a thick commercially-cultured soured cream. Minimum fat content 35%.

SOURDOUGH has a lightly sour taste from the yeast starter culture used to make the bread. A low-risen bread with a dense centre and crisp crust.

SUGAR
caster also known as superfine or finely granulated table sugar.
dark brown a moist, dark brown sugar with a rich distinctive full flavour coming from natural molasses syrup.
light brown a soft, finely granulated sugar retaining molasses for its characteristic colour and flavour.
white a coarsely granulated table sugar, also known as crystal sugar.

SULTANAS dried grapes, also known as golden raisins.

TAMARI see sauces.

TAMARIND CONCENTRATE the distillation of tamarind pulp into a condensed, compacted paste with a sweet-sour, slightly astringent taste. Thick and purple-black, it requires no soaking or straining. Found in Asian food stores and supermarkets.

TOFU also known as bean curd, an off-white, custard-like product made from the "milk" of crushed soya beans; comes fresh as soft or firm. Leftover fresh tofu can be refrigerated in water (which is changed daily) for up to 4 days.
silken tofu refers to the method by which it is made – where it is strained through silk.

TOMATOES
egg also called plum or roma; these are smallish, oval-shaped tomatoes much used in Italian cooking or salads.
paste triple-concentrated tomato puree.
puree canned pureed tomatoes (not tomato paste). Substitute with fresh peeled and pureed tomatoes.

TORTILLAS thin, round unleavened bread originating in Mexico. Two kinds are available, one made from wheat flour and the other from corn.

TURMERIC, GROUND a member of the ginger family, its root is dried and ground, resulting in the rich yellow powder that gives many Indian dishes their characteristic yellow colour. It is intensely pungent in taste but not hot.

VANILLA EXTRACT made by extracting the flavour from the vanilla bean pod; the pods are soaked, usually in alcohol, to capture the authentic flavour.

VINEGAR
balsamic made from the juice of Trebbiano grapes; it is a deep rich brown colour with a sweet and sour flavour.
white balsamic is a clear and lighter version of balsamic vinegar; it has a fresh, sweet, clean taste.
brown malt made from fermented malt and beech shavings.
cider (apple cider) made from fermented apples.
white made from the spirit of cane sugar.
white wine made from a blend of white wines.

WALNUTS a rich, flavourful nut. Should be plump and firm, not shrivelled or soft. Has a high oil content, so store in the fridge. Pecans can be substituted.

WHITE SWEET POTATO is less sweet than kumara; has an earthy flavour. It has a purple flesh beneath its white skin.

YOGURT we use plain yogurt unless otherwise indicated.

ZUCCHINI also known as courgette; small green, yellow or white vegetable belonging to the squash family.

Conversion Chart

MEASURES

One Australian metric measuring cup holds approximately 250ml; one Australian metric tablespoon holds 20ml; one Australian metric teaspoon holds 5ml.

The difference between one country's measuring cups and another's is within a two- or three-teaspoon variance, and will not affect your cooking results. North America, New Zealand and the United Kingdom use a 15ml tablespoon.

All cup and spoon measurements are level. The most accurate way of measuring dry ingredients is to weigh them. When measuring liquids, use a clear glass or plastic jug with the metric markings.

We use large eggs with an average weight of 60g.

DRY MEASURES

METRIC	IMPERIAL
15g	½oz
30g	1oz
60g	2oz
90g	3oz
125g	4oz (¼lb)
155g	5oz
185g	6oz
220g	7oz
250g	8oz (½lb)
280g	9oz
315g	10oz
345g	11oz
375g	12oz (¾lb)
410g	13oz
440g	14oz
470g	15oz
500g	16oz (1lb)
750g	24oz (1½lb)
1kg	32oz (2lb)

LIQUID MEASURES

METRIC	IMPERIAL
30ml	1 fluid oz
60ml	2 fluid oz
100ml	3 fluid oz
125ml	4 fluid oz
150ml	5 fluid oz
190ml	6 fluid oz
250ml	8 fluid oz
300ml	10 fluid oz (½ pint)
500ml	16 fluid oz
600ml	20 fluid oz (1 pint)
1000ml (1 litre)	1¾ pints

LENGTH MEASURES

METRIC	IMPERIAL
3mm	⅛in
6mm	¼in
1cm	½in
2cm	¾in
2.5cm	1in
5cm	2in
6cm	2½in
8cm	3in
10cm	4in
13cm	5in
15cm	6in
18cm	7in
20cm	8in
23cm	9in
25cm	10in
28cm	11in
30cm	12in (1ft)

OVEN TEMPERATURES

These oven temperatures are only a guide for conventional ovens. For fan-forced ovens, check the manufacturer's manual.

	°C (CELSIUS)	°F (FAHRENHEIT)	GAS MARK
Very slow	120	250	½
Slow	150	275-300	1-2
Moderately slow	160	325	3
Moderate	180	350-375	4-5
Moderately hot	200	400	6
Hot	220	425-450	7-8
Very hot	240	475	9

Index

Published in 2010 by ACP Books, Sydney
ACP Books are published by ACP Magazines
a division of PBL Media Pty Limited

ACP BOOKS

General manager Christine Whiston
Editor-in-chief Susan Tomnay
Creative director & designer Hieu Chi Nguyen
Art director Hannah Blackmore
Senior editor Wendy Bryant
Food director Pamela Clark
Sales & rights director Brian Cearnes
Marketing manager Bridget Cody
Senior business analyst Rebecca Varela
Circulation manager Jama Mclean
Operations manager David Scotto
Production manager Victoria Jefferys

Published by ACP Books, a division of
ACP Magazines Ltd, 54 Park St, Sydney;
GPO Box 4088, Sydney, NSW 2001.
phone (02) 9282 8618; fax (02) 9267 9438.

acpbooks@acpmagazines.com.au;
www.acpbooks.com.au

Printed by Toppan Printing Co, China.

Australia Distributed by Network Services,
phone +61 2 9282 8777; fax +61 2 9264 3278;
networkweb@networkservicescompany.com.au
United Kingdom Distributed by Australian Consolidated Press (UK),
phone (01604) 642 200;
fax (01604) 642 300; books@acpuk.com
New Zealand Distributed by Netlink Distribution Company,
phone (9) 366 9966; ask@ndc.co.nz
South Africa Distributed by PSD Promotions,
phone (27 11) 392 6065/6/7; fax (27 11) 392 6079/80; orders@psdprom.co.za
Canada Distributed by Publishers Group Canada
phone (800) 663 5714; fax (800) 565 3770; service@raincoast.com

Slow-cooker / food director Pamela Clark.
ISBN: 978 186396 938 3 (pbk.)
Notes: Includes index.
Subjects: Electric cookery, Slow.
Other Authors/Contributors: Clark, Pamela.
Also Titled: Australian women's weekly.
Dewey Number: 641.5884
© ACP Magazines Ltd 2010
ABN 18 053 273 546

Recipe development Nicole Jennings,
Rebecca Squadrito, Cathie Lonnie
Nutritional information Rebecca Squadrito
Photographer Ian Wallace
Stylist Louise Pickford
Food preparation Rebecca Squadrito
Cover Creamy turkey stew with mustard, page 50

The publishers would like to thank the following for props used in photography: Alfresco Emporium,
ELTON Group, Favourite Things, Mud Australia, Village Living.

Scanpan cookware is used in the AWW Test Kitchen.

To order books
phone 136 116 (within Australia) or
order online at www.acpbooks.com.au
Send recipe enquiries to:
recipeenquiries@acpmagazines.com.au